# NORTH AFRICA
# AND ITALY
## 1942 – 1944

# BLITZKRIEG

# NORTH AFRICA AND ITALY
## 1942 – 1944

## WILL FOWLER

Ian Allan
PUBLISHING

First published 2003

ISBN 0 7110 2948 2

© Will Fowler 2003

Published by Ian Allan Publishing
an imprint of Ian Allan Publishing Ltd, Hersham, Surrey KT12 4RG.

Printed by Ian Allan Printing Ltd, Hersham, Surrey KT12 4RG.

Code: 0310/A2

Designed by Casebourne Rose Design Associates Ltd

Illustrations by Mike Rose
Maps by Sue Casebourne

Picture Credits
All photographs with the following exceptions are from Bugle Archives.
IWM 6, 12 (top), 22, 23 (top), 27 (top), 36 (top), 64 (top), 67 (bottom), 74, 75, 84 (top), 86, 87, 88.
US National Archives 31, 34, 40, 55, 57, 65, 68, 70, 71, 80, 81, 84 (bottom), 85 (top), 90, 91.

***Blitzkrieg:*** Fast armoured and mechanised warfare supported by bombers and ground attack aircraft.

# CONTENTS

## EL ALAMEIN

6-27

The battle of El Alamein was the decisive 8th Army victory over the *Afrika Korps* that the British Prime Minister Churchill craved before the United States entered the war with landings in Morocco. Under General Bernard Montgomery the pursuit following the El Alamein victory was slow even though ULTRA intelligence showed the *Afrika Korps* was broken.

## THE SOFT UNDERBELLY

28-43

Churchill asserted that an attack on Fascist Italy would be an attack on the "soft underbelly" of the Italian/German Axis. What he and the British and American planners did not consider was that the Germans would move reinforcements rapidly down the peninsula.

## AEGEAN VICTORY

44-53

In 1943 the Italian-held islands off the Turkish coast were up for grabs. Churchill saw a chance to bring Turkey into the war on the side of the Allies and sent British troops to seize them. The Germans counter attacked and triumphed.

## THE GUSTAV LINE

54-77

The German defence of Monte Cassino and the containment of the landings at Anzio was a triumph of defensive fighting that at Anzio was close to becoming a victory. Under Field Marshal Kesselring they held the Allies until June 1944.

## THE ETERNAL CITY AND BEYOND

78-93

Rome fell on June 5, 1944 but the Allies had months of hard fighting ahead, as the Germans withdrew to new defensive lines.

INDEX 95–96

# EL ALAMEIN

*The German people, in company with myself, are following your heroic defensive struggle in Egypt with devout trust in your personal leadership and the bravery of the German and Italian troops who serve you. In your present situation you can have no other thought than to hold out, refuse to yield a step, and commit to the battle every weapon and every soldier who can be released from other duties.*

*Signal from Adolf Hitler to Field Marshal Erwin Rommel*
*13.30, November 3, 1942*

The Second Battle of Alamein began on the night of October 23, 1942, when the darkness was ripped apart by a bombardment of 1,000 British guns. The shellfire and attacks by the Desert Air Force smashed German and Italian positions and ripped up barbed wire and minefields. The 8th Army under General Bernard Montgomery then moved off to attack the joint German and Italian forces under Field Marshal Erwin Rommel at 21.30.

Rommel's positions were anchored on the

**ABOVE:** A British soldier armed with an SMLE rifle moves forward cautiously on a ridgeline.

**ABOVE:** *Afrika Korps* gunners load a 21cm Mörser 18 howitzer. The big gun could fire one 133kg round every two minutes.

sea in the north and the Qattara Depression, a salt marsh impassable to vehicles, in the south. Along this front were hills, ridges or depressions that were incorporated into the defences. From north to south the most significant were Kidney, Miteirya and Ruweisat Ridges with the Munassib Depression.

Rommel had positioned his German and Italian infantry so that the less reliable Italian troops were "corseted" by German troops on each flank. On the coast the XXI Corps was commanded by General Navarrini, in the centre was the XX Corps under General de Stephani and to the south X Corps under General Gioda.

**ABOVE:** Protected against the blowing desert sand by *Luftwaffe*-issue goggles, an aspirant officer in the *Afrika Korps* sits in a truck with his comrades.

## MEN, MACHINES AND MINES

Knowing that they were faced by extensive minefields, the "Devil's Gardens", the 8th Army deployed Modified Matilda II tanks. The robust chassis was the basis for the Scorpion mine-clearing flail system and 32 Matilda II Scorpions advanced at El Alamein clearing paths through the minefields. The flail consisted of a rotating drum mounted on arms forward of the tank. Weighted chains or "flails" were attached to the drum and as it rotated they thrashed the ground and exploded mines harmlessly in front of the tank. It was said that one Italian soldier surrendered to one of these terrifying, but actually unarmed, vehicles. On foot Royal Engineers equipped with electronic mine detectors also searched for mines, advancing paying out a white tape to show their path through the minefield. A cruder but essentially more reliable technique was to "prod" pushing a SMLE bayonet at an angle into the soil to feel if it bumped against the side casing of a buried mine. Other men with light wands advanced feeling for trip wire from S Mines. If the Engineers located a mine they placed a conical white folding fabric marker on top of it. It would then be destroyed or defused.

On the north the German 164th Light Division (Div) covered the coastal road and rail links that ran from Egypt into Tripolitania and Kidney Ridge. To the south the Italian *Trento* and *Littorio* Divs held the Miteirya Ridge with the *Bologna* Div to their right. The tough German *Ramcke Fallschirmbrigade* was south of Ruweisat Ridge with the Brescia Div to the right. The Italian *Folgore* Parachute Div held the flank on the Qattara Depression with the *Pavia* Div in reserve on the El Taqa Plateau and at the far south was the *"Kiel"* Battle Group.

In reserve ready to counter attack any break through Rommel held his armoured and mobile troops. To the north the 15th Panzer and *Littorio* Divs with the 90th Light Div were in depth at Gazala and in the south

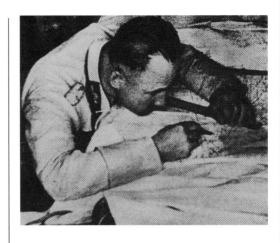

**ABOVE:** Field Marshal Erwin Rommel hunches over maps in a front-line command post. His radio orders were intercepted and decoded by an 8th Army ULTRA team and passed to Montgomery.

**LEFT:** Ammunition is broken out of its wicker containers and brought forward by an *Afrika Korps* 15cm sFH 18 howitzer crew.

**ABOVE:** A dummy 25 Pounder position constructed by the 8th Army. Both sides used deception schemes to conceal their positions and movements.

the veteran 21st Panzer and Ariete Divs.

In the darkness of October 23 the British XXX Corps under General Oliver Leese and the X Corps under General Lumsden began to fight through these formidable minefields and defences. In the first phase of the attack, Operation Lightfoot, the infantry of the 9th Australian, 51st Highland, New Zealand and 1st South African Divs were to make the initial break in through the deep defences. This would allow the 1st Armoured and 10th Armoured Divs to exploit westwards through

## CAPTIVE SHERMAN

During the fighting in Tunisia soldiers of the *Afrika Korps* captured an M4 Sherman and writing in *Die Wehrmacht* in March 1943 German Army correspondent Eberhard Schulz described the arrival of the tank in Tunis. It had been captured by a reconnaissance patrol from a Panzer regiment in the hills of Sbeitla on a foggy morning on February 22. The German crew then drove it for 338km (210 miles) over four and a half days "which" wrote Schulz "testifies well to the overall march capacity of this steel colossus" to the port of Sfax. Here it was loaded onto a ship and "now after many intermediate stops, this star of American armament has arrived at its destination, a proving ground near Berlin, in the hands of arms experts who are evaluating its combat efficiency and durability. Preliminary investigation in Tunisia had already revealed that it is not a bad product." (For M4 Sherman specifications see *Blitzkrieg* 4).

**ABOVE:** German troops examine another captured vehicle, a US M3 Light Tank.

**ABOVE:** Dust is kicked up as an *Afrika Korps* 7.62cm Pak 36(r) anti-tank gun opens fire. The gun was a modified captured Russian weapon.

two corridors in Operation Supercharge.

To the south the XIII Corps under General Brian Horrocks launched spoiling attacks on October 25 against the Italian *Folgore* Div.

In overall command of British and Commonwealth forces in the theatre was General Harold Alexander who had been appointed commander in chief in the Middle East in August 1942.

Montgomery had ordered an elaborate deception operation to convince Rommel that an attack could be expected from the south – a conventional approach that would allow

**LEFT:** Eye pressed to the sights, an *Afrika Korps* gunner lays an anti-tank gun. Engagement ranges in the desert were further than those of Europe.

the 8th Army to hook right into position behind the Axis forces in the north. To sustain this impression dummy depots had been constructed along with fake tanks and guns. This ploy would ensure that the 21st Panzer and the Italian *Ariete* Divs would remain in the south for a critical seven days during the battle.

Rommel, who was suffering from jaundice and other ailments caused by life in the desert, had flown to Germany on sick leave on September 23 and was due to return to Africa on October 25. Command of German and Italian forces in Africa was therefore delegated to General Georg Stumme.

On the second day of the battle, Stumme driving to the front came under heavy fire and as his driver took evasive action the general was thrown from the vehicle, suffered a heart attack and died. (For further

**ABOVE:** A captured 8.8cm Flak with its shield showing the "kills" it had scored against a variety of targets including a ship.

**ABOVE:** A German soldier takes cover behind a stone sangar. Though some positions were dug, others were constructed with stones and rocks.

# FIELD MARSHAL BERNARD MONTGOMERY

Bernard Law Montgomery was born in London on November 17, 1887, and educated at the Royal Military College, Sandhurst. He entered the British army in 1908 and served in World War I in the Royal Warwickshire Rgt where he was severely wounded and awarded the DSO. In World War II he returned to France in 1939 commanding the 3rd Div and took part in the withdrawal to Dunkerque in 1940. He was a small man with a rather piping voice. As a non-smoker and strict abstainer he was a rather austere figure in the British army. He came to prominence when commanding the 8th Army in North Africa where he defeated Rommel's *Afrika Korps* at El Alamein in October 1942. Despite having accurate ULTRA intelligence on the very poor state of the *Afrika Korps,* he was reluctant to press them following the victory at El Alamein. He commanded the 8th Army in the invasion of Sicily and Italy in 1943. In January 1944 he was recalled for the final stages of the invasion of northwest Europe. At D-Day he commanded the 21st Army Group composed of the American 1st Army and British 2nd Army. In August 1944, he was promoted to Field Marshal and led the Anglo Canadian forces to final victory in 1945, accepting the surrender of German forces in north west Germany at his HQ at Lüneberg Heath on May 3, 1945.

In 1946 Montgomery was created Viscount and appointed Chief of the Imperial General Staff (CIGS). He was Deputy Supreme Commander of the North Atlantic Treaty Organisation (NATO) forces from 1951 to 1958. Montgomery died in Alton, Hampshire, on March 25, 1976.

**LEFT:** A dumpy German 7.5cm leIG 18 infantry support gun in action. It weighed 400kg (880lb), and fired a 6kg (13.2lb) shell out to 3,550m (3,870yds), and was developed from World War I experience.

**ABOVE:** A ground-strafing Messerschmitt Bf109 fighter flies over an RAF Spitfire. Though the *Luftwaffe* did achieve air parity at times in 1943, it was largely on the defensive.

**BELOW:** A sunshade protects the cockpit of a Bf109 as ground crew and pilot keep cool under the wing. Heat and dust played havoc with engines and controls.

**ABOVE:** The superb tan and brown camouflage on a *Luftwaffe* Bf109 (trop) fighter matches the sand and scrub as it flies low across the North African desert.

information on Stumme see Blitzkrieg 5.)

The battle soon became a grim slogging match as the superior forces under Montgomery attempted to break through the thick defences. On October 25 Rommel was back in command and realised that the 9th Australian Div was clawing its way into the Axis defences. He committed the 15th Panzer Div against the Australians on October 26. Montgomery called a halt to operations. There was heavy fighting at the Miteririya and Kidney Ridges where Axis attacks were beaten off. On November 2 Montgomery launched Supercharge just south of the Australian salient and Rommel contacted Hitler requesting permission for a limited withdrawal. As on the Eastern Front, the order from the *Führer* was to "stand fast".

By November 4, when he was down to 30 tanks, Rommel was forced to retreat. Montgomery did not press the *Afrika Korps* as it withdrew despite detailed ULTRA information about its weakened state. The German withdrawal was like a roll call of former battles, but this time there would be no return match. On November 7 Mersa Matruh fell after two days of heavy rain that had impeded movement. Bardia was captured on November 11, Tobruk two days later and Gazala on November 13. Benghazi fell on November 20. Rommel held the line at El Agheila from November 24 to December 13 and withdrew before being outflanked and pushed back to Sirte on Christmas Day. Mussolini demanded that Rommel should hold Buerat to the last. The *Afrika Korps* and Italian forces held it from December 26 to January 13 before withdrawing in the face of a planned attack by the 8th Army. On January 23 the British entered Tripoli and that day Rommel pulled back into Tunisia.

The Battle of Alamein had cost the Axis approximately 50,000 casualties of whom 30,000 were prisoners, largely Italians who lacked the transport to escape. British losses were 13,560. Rommel, who had previously admired and respected Hitler, now felt that his loyalties were now to Germany and no longer the *Führer*.

## GENERAL GEORGE SMITH PATTON

Born in San Gabriel, California, in 1885, Patton was educated at the United States Military Academy. He was commissioned a second lieutenant in 1909 and served as ADC to General Joseph John "Black Jack" Pershing on Pershing's expedition to Mexico in 1917. In France during World War I, Patton established a tank training school and commanded a tank brigade. In 1942 and 1943, during World War II, he commanded US forces in Morocco, Tunisia, and Sicily. He was relieved of his command in Sicily following widespread protests in the United States and Mediterranean over the "soldier slapping incident".

While visiting the 93rd Evacuation Hospital at Sant Agata on August 10, 1943 to decorate wounded soldiers in his command he encountered an unwounded soldier. He asked him what he was doing in hospital and the soldier replied "It's my nerves. I can't stand the shelling anymore." Enraged Patton slapped the man with his gloves shouting "Shut up that Goddamned crying. I won't have brave men here who have been shot seeing a yellow bastard crying." Pulling his pistol from its holster he added: "I ought to shoot you myself, you Goddamned whimpering coward."

Early in 1944 Patton was given command of the 3rd Army. He remained controversial throughout the war for his personal flamboyance, uncompromising standards outspokenness, and aggressive leadership. Soldiers commented on his nickname "Blood and Guts" – "Our blood, his guts".

In the summer of 1944 the 3rd Army broke out of Normandy and advanced rapidly across France; in March 1945 it crossed the Rhine into Germany and also moved towards Austria. After the war Patton served as military governor of Bavaria, but because of criticism of his lenient policy towards the former enemy, he was relieved of the post. He was named head of the 15th Army late in 1945, shortly before he was fatally injured in a traffic accident.

# SdKfz 2 *LEICHTE KETTEN-KRAD* NSU HK-101

Originally designed for the German airborne forces as an airportable towing vehicle for light trailers and guns like the Pak 35/36, after Crete the Ketten-Krad was more widely adopted. It had storage lockers and two rear-ward facing seats. The driver sat on a motorcycle style seat and steered through the single front wheel. Production that began in 1940 ceased in 1944. It was used as a supply vehicle over rough terrain.

| | |
|---|---|
| Armament: | n/a |
| Armour: | n/a |
| Crew: | 3 |
| Weight: | 1,200kg (1 ton) |
| Hull length: | 2.74m (8ft 11in) |
| Width: | 1m (3ft 3in) |
| Height: | 1.01m (3ft 3in) |
| Engine: | One Opel Olympia 38 petrol engine developing 36hp |
| Road speed: | 80km/h (49.7mph) |
| Range: | 100km (62.5miles) |

MEDITERRANEAN SEA

Main movements of the Afrika Korps

8th Army attacks

Axis enclaves

Axis minefields

El Daba

Ghazal

90 LT DIV
28 Oct

Sidi abd el Rahman

XV PZ DIV & LITTORIO DIV

XI AUST DIV
51st H DIV

Führer XXX CORPS (Leese)

El Alamein

Führer X CORPS (Lumsden)

Kidney Ridge

Rahman Track

TRENTO DIV

Miteirya Ridge

1 ARMD DIV

10 ARMD DIV

BOLOGNA DIV

4 IND DIV

Ruweisat Ridge

Western edge of 8th Army minefields

Führer DAK HQ

XXI PZ DIV & ARIETE DIV

BRESCIA DIV

Führer XIII CORPS (Horrocks)

44 DIV

7 ARMD DIV

Naqb Abu Dweis

El Taqa Plateau

FOLGORE DIV

PAVIA DIV

1 FREE FRENCH BDE

Qattara Depression

**ABOVE:** The battle of El Alamein was a tough fight even though General Bernard Montgomery and the 8th Army had the advantage of superior forces and ULTRA intelligence.

# BLITZKRIEG

**RIGHT:** Morose US soldiers captured at Kasserine in the *Afrika Korps'* final counter attack in Tunisia are marched to the rear.

**ABOVE:** The burned out wreckage of a USAAF Lockheed P-38F Lightning shot down in North Africa. The fighter bomber was nicknamed by the Germans "The Two Tailed Devil".

For Churchill the victory was particularly significant after over three years of defeats in Europe, Africa and the Far East. The British and Commonwealth had scored a major victory even before the United States had committed ground forces to the war. He had cabled General Alexander on September 17 demanding that the attack be launched before the end of September and he only

**LEFT:** Victor and vanquished. A *Luftwaffe* fighter pilot, holder of the Knight's Cross, with the USAAF Lockheed P-38F Lightning pilot he has shot down.

grudgingly accepted Alexander's explanation that the 8th Army required more training but that an attack in October would be successful.

From 1943 onwards Churchill knew that the US would become the senior partner in the Allied war in the West. On November 8, 1942, the first moves in this change of command took place with the Anglo-American Torch landings. They took place at Morocco and Algeria, and the Germans and Italians were caught between two armies. Three Task Forces, respectively Western under General George Patton, Centre under General Lloyd Fredenhall and the Eastern under General Charles Ryder. The Western had sailed directly from the United States and landed at three points in Morocco. The

**LEFT AND BELOW:** A pause in the march into captivity for GIs captured in Tunisia. Film and photographs of American prisoners helped to convince the German public that, despite some setbacks, the *Afrika Korps* was still fighting effectively in Africa against the Allies.

## ME323E-2 *GIGANT* (GIANT)

The powered development of the Me321 heavy transport glider, the Me323, entered service in 1942 on the cross-Mediterranean routes supplying troops in North Africa. They suffered heavily in the Tunisian campaign in 1943. On the Eastern Front they were used in the Crimea for supply and casualty evacuation and later in the Baltic for logistic support. The distinctive clamshell nose doors which gave access to the cargo hold were big enough to take a 15cm gun and half-track prime mover.

| | |
|---|---|
| Type: | Heavy transport |
| Crew/Accommodation: | 7/11 |
| Power Plant: | Six 1,140hp Gnome-Rhône 14N 48/49 |
| Performance: | Maximum speed at 3,000m (9,840ft) 220km/h (137mph) Normal range 1,200km (745miles) |
| Weights: | Empty 29,600kg (65,260lb) Maximum 45,000kg (99,210lb) |
| Dimensions: | Wing span 55m (180ft 5in) Length 28.5m (93ft 6in) Height 9.6m (31ft 6in) |
| Armament: | One 20mm MG 151 cannon in each of two upper wing turrets; one 13mm MG 131 machine gun each at rear of flight deck, two in nose-door, and four (fore and aft) beam positions; plus provision for additional hand-held 7.9mm MG 34 machine guns firing from hold windows. |

## HAWKER HURRICANE MK IID

The tank-busting Hurricane IID equipped five squadrons in North Africa and three in Burma as well as equipping the squadrons of the Indian Air Force in Burma. The Mk IIA that had entered service in 1940 had equipped two RAF squadrons that had operated in Northern Russia in 1941. By the end of the war the Mk II and IV would equip a total of 98 RAF squadrons.

| | |
|---|---|
| Type: | Fighter and anti-tank ground attack aircraft |
| Crew: | 1 |
| Power Plant: | One 1,280hp Rolls-Royce Merlin XX |
| Performance: | Maximum speed at 5,486m (18,000 ft) 529km/h (329mph) Maximum range 1,480 km (920 miles) |
| Weights: | Empty 2,569kg (5,658lb) Maximum 3,649kg (8,044lb) |
| Dimensions: | Wing span 12.19m (40ft) Length 9.81m (32ft 2in) Height 3.98m (13ft 1in) |
| Armament: | Two 40mm Rolls-Royce B.F. or Vickers Type S anti-tank guns in underwing fairings; two .303in Browning machine guns. |

# BRISTOL BEAUFIGHTER T.F. MK X

The Beaufighter T.F. Mk X was the maritime strike version of this versatile fighter bomber and was employed not only against enemy shipping, attempting to run the air and sea blockade on Occupied Europe, but also against German U-Boats. Rockets were the most effective weapon against both shipping and submarines, but torpedoes could also be employed against surface vessels. In 1945 Beaufighter T.F. Mk Xs of Nos 236 and 254 squadrons were directed onto U-Boats probably through ULTRA intelligence, and sank five in 48 hours in March 1945. Beaufighters fitted with nose-mounted airborne radar proved a formidable night interceptor.

| | |
|---|---|
| Type: | Anti-shipping strike fighter |
| Crew: | 2 or 3 |
| Power Plant: | Two 1,770hp Bristol Hercules XVII |
| Performance: | Maximum speed at 3,962m (13,000ft) 488km/h (303mph) Maximum range 2,366km (1,470 miles) |
| Weights: | Empty 7,072kg (15,592lb) Maximum 11,521kg (25,400lb) |
| Dimensions: | Wing span 17.63m (57ft 10in) Length 12.7m (41ft 8in) Height 4.82m (15ft 10in) |
| Armament: | Four 20mm Hispano cannon in nose; one 303in Vickers K gun in dorsal position; one 748kg (1,650lb) or 965kg (2,127lb) torpedo; two 113.4kg (250lb) bombs or eight 41kg (90lb) rockets. |

**BELOW:** German paratroops talk to a sentry by a burning USAAF Lockheed P-38F Lightning. Given that ammunition might "cook off" – explode in the fire – this is a patently posed photograph.

Centre sailing from the Clyde in the United Kingdom landed to the west and east of Oran and the Eastern, which had also sailed from the UK, landed at three points around Algiers. The French resisted the landings and inflicted casualties, but secret contacts between Admiral François Darlan, commanding Vichy forces in North Africa, and the Allies led to an armistice being signed on November 11. On that day German forces entered the area of southern France that had remained unoccupied since 1940.

From November 9 the Germans quickly flew reinforcements into El Aouina airport in Tunisia from Sicily in a bridgehead that used huge Me323 Gigants as well as Ju52 transports. A new force in Africa, the 5th Panzer

Armee under General Jürgen von Arnim, was established. It would be composed of 100,000 good-quality troops and would receive the first Tiger tanks.

With fresh troops new equipment and inspired leadership the Germans held out until May 11, 1943 and on February 19, in his final throw in North Africa, Rommel would defeat US forces at Kasserine Pass. This counter attack was not on the scale of the *Blitzkrieg* battles of 1939-42, but like the fighting in Sicily and at Anzio on the Italian mainland saw German tanks and infantry working in concert. In the Mediterranean theatre, as in the USSR, German forces knew the value of counter attacks to recover lost territory or buy time during withdrawals. The exception would be the small-scale actions fought in the autumn of 1943 at the Aegean islands of Kos and Leros – a German victory but merely a distraction for the Allies.

By late January, with the 1st Army pushing into Tunisia, von Arnim and Rommel were pressing Field Marshal Albert Kesselring, the *Oberbefehlshaber Süd* (OB) Commander-in-Chief South, for permission to counter attack. Rommel, ever ambitious, wanted to launch a decisive thrust through Tebessa and into the rear of the 1st Army, while von Arnim, aware of the poor supply situation, favoured spoiling attacks to buy time. Kesselring allowed both commanders to launch their own operations. To the east the *Afrika Korps* was in a position to delay the 8th Army on the Mareth Line.

**BELOW**: A British Military Policeman at a junction directs traffic in Tunisia. In the background despatch riders wait by their motorcycles.

**ABOVE:** A British sapper uses an electronic mine detector to locate mines near the Medjez-Tebourba road, Longstop Hill, Tunisia in April 1943.

This was a line built by the French before the war to protect French administered Tunisia from attack by Italy that held Libya. The Mareth Line used natural features like Wadi Akarit as well as high ground to enhance the effectiveness of the bunkers that covered the approaches.

On February 14 von Arnim in Operation Spring Wind hit the French and Americans at Sidi Bou Zid, and a day later Rommel launched Operation Morning Wind at Gafsa against the US II Corps under General

**RIGHT:** Breaching the Geneva Convention, a page from the German multilingual propaganda magazine *Signal* shows US Army officers and men captured in Tunisia.

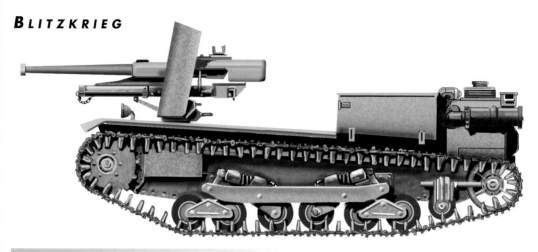

## 90/53 SEMOVENTE

Built by Ansaldo on a M14-41 tank chassis, the 90/53 Semovente was armed with a 90mm Model 41 AA gun as an SP anti-tank gun. The British put the performance of the Model 41 as equivalent to the German 8.8cm Flak 18. Only 24 were built and these were destroyed in the fighting in Sicily. The size of the gun made it necessary to mount it in the open, which exposed the crew. Another drawback was the limited load of six rounds that could be carried.

| | |
|---|---|
| Armament: | 1 90mm gun 90/53 Mod 39 |
| Armour: | 40mm maximum |
| Crew: | 4 |
| Weight: | 17,000kg (16.73 tons) |
| Hull length: | 5.28m (17ft 4in) |
| Width: | 2.26m (7ft 4in) |
| Height: | 2.15m (7ft 1in) |
| Engine: | SPA 15-Tm, 8 cylinder diesel 145bhp at 1,800 rpm |
| Road speed: | 30km/h (18mph) |
| Range: | 150km (93 miles) |

**RIGHT:** The two German counter attacks in Tunisia in 1943, Operations Morning Wind and Spring Wind that climaxed in the battle of Kasserine. The attacks hit the inexperienced US 5th Army, but though they captured men and destroyed weapons the operations only bought time for the *Afrika Korps* and 5th *Panzerarmee*.

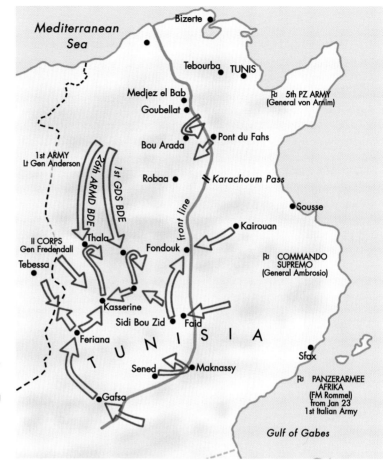

**LEFT:** A camouflaged *Afrika Korps* 15cm K18 howitzer at full recoil. Firing a 43kg (94.6lb) shell the K18 had a maximum range of 24,825m (27,060yds).

Fredenhall. Von Arnim, using a double envelopment manoeuvre, quickly captured Sidi Bou Zid. Rommel seized Gafsa and advanced to Feriana while von Arnim made for Sbeitla. On February 17 the Afrika Korps under Rommel seized Feriana and drove for the Kasserine Pass. The 5th *Panzerarmee* captured Sbeitla on February 18 and sent a force north-east to Fondouk.

On February 19 the Anglo-American forces received a much needed tonic when General Sir Harold Alexander took command of the newly created 18th Army Group that consisted of the 1st and 8th Armies. He ordered Lt General Kenneth Anderson commanding the 1st Army to hold all the exits

from the mountains into western Tunisia. On the same day Rommel seized Kasserine Pass, albeit after two days of heavy fighting. British reinforcements began to arrive to cover the Thala-Kasserine road.

Following the defeat at Kasserine the German multi-lingual propaganda magazine *Signal* featured photographs of the shocked and tired faces of US soldiers as they were marched into captivity. In a cruel pun on the title of John Ford's 1941 Hollywood triumph *How Green Was My Valley*, a film about a Welsh coal mining community, British veterans of the 8th Army quipped: "How green are our Allies".

On February 20 Rommel was rebuffed at

Sbiba and swung towards Thala but was halted there. He realised that Morning Wind had run its course. The Commando Supremo General Ambrosio ordered him to turn south the stop the 8th Army. Von Arnim was to distract the 1st Army with attacks code named Ox Head as Rommel launched Operation Capri against Medenine. Montgomery, alerted by ULTRA, had already anticipated the German attacks as von Arnim launched a series of attacks from the coast south to Bou Arada. What became known as the Battle of Medenine took place on March 6 and in it the 8th Army halted the *Afrika Korps*. On the same day that Montgomery won the Battle of Medenine, in which the Axis lost 55 tanks and 500 dead, on Eisenhower's orders, General Patton replaced Fredenhall in command of II Corps. It would be the first indication that though Eisenhower might be genial and diplomatic, he could also be very firm if subordinates failed him and the US Army.

Following this success at Kasserine, which was to be his last victory in World War II, Rommel, who was suffering from ill health,

was replaced by von Arnim as Commander-in-Chief of the Axis forces on March 9. If the "Desert Fox" had been obliged to surrender, German morale, seriously battered, would have been even more badly hurt.

Montgomery attacked the Mareth line on March 20. The Italians and German forces were fighting with ferocious tenacity, but the firepower and numbers of the Anglo-American armies, who had been joined by the French, squeezed the Axis northwards into Tunisia towards Cape Bon. On May 7 the port of Bizerta and the capital Tunis were captured, and on May 11 the 10th Panzer Division fought its last battle against the British 6th Armoured Division on Cape Bon. The OKW reported that a *Luftwaffe* Flak division used its last remaining shells in an action that destroyed 37 Allied tanks. These brave reports, however, could not disguise

**BELOW:** American and French officers and dignitaries take the salute as men of the French Foreign Legion parade in Algiers. French troops from Algeria would fight from 1943-45.

**LEFT:** Following the surrender in Tunisia, a British Military Policeman checks the paybook of an Italian soldier from the *Bersaglieri* with his distinctive black cockerel insignia on his sun helmet.

**BELOW:** *Generalleutnant* Gustav von Vaerst averts his head from a photographer as senior *Afrika Korps* officers are flown in following the surrender in May 1943. Von Vaerst took over temporary command of the *Afrika Korps* when *General der Panzertruppe* Nehring was wounded on August 31, 1942.

the fact that this was a defeat on the same scale as Stalingrad.

The final victory in Tunisia had cost the Allies 75,000 casualties, but the Axis had suffered 300,000 casualties of whom 240,000 were prisoners. A few hundred soldiers had escaped by air to Sicily, but huge quantities of military equipment were captured. At Hamman Lif the British captured intact a depot with 4.5 million litres (1.18 million gallons) of fuel, and artillery and ammunition. In Bizerta the US II Corps seized a depot with 12,190,000kg (12,000 tons) of military stores and rations.

It was the end of the *Afrika Korps*.

Alexander signalled Churchill: "We are masters of the North African shore."

The next move by the Allies seemed obvious. An attack on Sicily, the mainland territory of the Fascist adversary. Churchill urged it, describing Italy as "the soft underbelly" of the Axis. In fact it would prove remarkably tough and the fighting would last from July 9, 1943 to May 2, 1945.

# THE SOFT UNDERBELLY

*A violent battle is underway along the coast of eastern Italy where Italian and German troops are vigorously combating enemy forces who have landed there and are bravely withstanding their pressure. Enemy aerial forces are active. Axis fighter planes have shot down 22 enemy aircraft, anti-aircraft guns 9.*

*Italian Forces High CommandSunday July 11, 1943*

The weight of the defence of Italy fell on the capable shoulders of Albert Kesselring, a *Luftwaffe* Field Marshal, who became an able land commander. Rommel had commented in a letter to his wife that he thought that Kesselring had been given the command because he had shown more optimism about holding Italy.

Under Kesselring the Germans fought a series of actions on defence lines across the

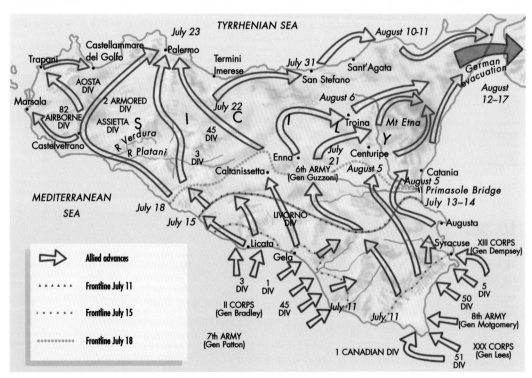

**ABOVE:** Operation Husky, the Anglo-American amphibious and airborne landings in Sicily in 1943. Though the British 8th Army under General Montgomery was tasked with the capture of Messina, the US 7th Army under General Patton raced it to the port, reaching it on August 17.

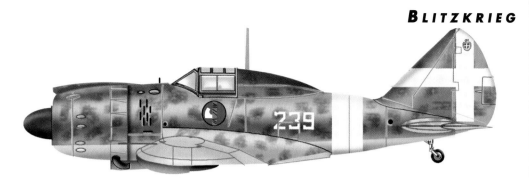

# REGGIANE RE.2002 *ARIETE* (RAM)

Reverting to a radial engine, Reggiane delivered the Re2002 to the Italian Air Force in 1942. Based in Sicily, equipping one assault *Stormo* and two *Gruppi*, it opposed the Allied landings in 1943. By the time of the Armistice only 16 aircraft were still flying. It was subsequently used in small numbers by both the *Aeronautica Nazionale Repubblicana* in the north and the Italian Cobeligerent Air Force. The *Luftwaffe* also used them in anti-partisan operations in France in 1944.

| | |
|---|---|
| Type: | Fighter |
| Crew: | 1 |
| Power Plant: | One 1,180hp Piaggio P.XIX RC 45 Turbine B |
| Performance: | Maximum speed at 5,500m (18,045ft) 530km/h (329mph) Normal range 1,100km (684 miles) |
| Weights: | Empty 2,390kg (5,269lb) Loaded 3,240kg (7,143lb) |
| Dimensions: | Wing span 11m (36ft 1in) Length 8.165m (26ft 9in) Height 3.15m (10ft 4in) |
| Armament: | two 12.7 Breda-SAFAT machine guns in wings; max bomb load 950kg (2,095lb) or one torpedo under fuselage plus 320kg (706lb) bombs underwing. |

# LOCKHEED P-38F LIGHTNING

The radical twin rail-boom heavily armed fighter entered service in August 1941. Its first kill was a year later when an Iceland based Lightning shot down a FW200 over the Atlantic. Two USAAF groups that had arrived in Britain were transferred to North Africa as part of the 12th Air Force. They saw action there and in Sicily and Italy as part of the 12th AF and later the 15th AF. One captured aircraft, a P-38E, was evaluated by the *Luftwaffe*.

| | |
|---|---|
| Type: | Long-range fighter/fighter bomber |
| Crew: | 1 |
| Power Plant: | Two 1,250hp Allison V-1710-49/53 |
| Performance: | Maximum speed at 1,524m (5,000ft) 558km/h (347mph) Maximum range 2,293km (1,425 miles) |
| Weights: | Empty 6,169kg (13,600lb) Maximum 9,070kg (20,000lb) |
| Dimensions: | Wing span 15.85m (52ft) Length 11.52m (37ft 10in) Height 2.99m (9ft 10in) |
| Armament: | One 20mm Hispano cannon, four .5in Browning machine guns in nose; max bomb load 907kg (2,000lb) |

# FIELD MARSHAL ALBERT KESSELRING

Born in Marktsheft, Bavaria, on November 20, 1885, he was the child of a middle class family. In 1904 he joined the Army as a probationer in the 2nd Bavarian Foot Artillery. In World War I Kesselring served on the Western Front for two years and then joined the artillery staff. In 1917 he was appointed to the General Staff and posted to a division on the Eastern Front. In 1918 he held appointments on the Staff at Corps and Army level under Prinz Rupprecht. In 1936 he was made chief of the General Staff of the *Luftwaffe*. Under his command *Luftflotte* I supported the Army in 1939 in Poland and 1940 in Flanders.

Kesselring was promoted Field Marshal in 1940 at the end of the campaign in France and awarded the *Ritterkreuz* (Knight's Cross). From December 1941 to March 1945 Kesselring was *Oberbefehlshaber Süd* (OB), Commander-in-Chief South and Army Group C, covering the Mediterranean and Italy.

Kesselring's personal charm enabled him to make friends with senior Italian commanders and even Benito Mussolini as well as the hard, driving commander of the *Afrika Korps*, Erwin Rommel. However, when the *Luftwaffe* Field Marshal urged caution as Rommel pushed eastwards towards Cairo in June 1942 he found himself under attack not only from Hitler but also from Mussolini. On October 23, 1944 Kesselring was severely injured in a road accident. Following successful brain surgery he took up his OB South post again on January 15, 1945. From March 25 to May 6, 1945 Kesselring was responsible for combat operations in western Germany, he introduced himself to the staff of his demoralised HQ staff in Germany with a broad grin and the words

"Good morning gentlemen, I am the new V3". His optimism in some tough and difficult situations earned him the nickname "Smiling Al". On May 6, 1947 he was found guilty for ordering the execution of 335 Italian civilians as a reprisal for an attack by Italian partisans and condemned to death. The sentence was commuted to life imprisonment in October 1947 and he was pardoned and released on October 23, 1952. He died in Bad Nauheim on July 16, 1960.

**ABOVE:** Hitler and Mussolini watch as Jodl displays maps with Keitel in the background.

Italian peninsula. Hitler had ordered that a line should be held south of Rome and on the Gustav Line that incorporated the River Garigliano, the Apennines and the monastery of Monte Cassino. The Germans would hold the Allies from January to May 1944.

Kesselring realised that the longer he delayed the Allies south of Rome, the longer he prevented USAAF and RAF bombers from operating from bases in Italy where they could strike targets in Austria and southern Germany. Work on the Gustav Line began as soon as the Allies landed at Salerno and Kesselring ordered his troops to conduct a fighting withdrawal through the autumn.

An indicator of the weight of Allied airpower that would be deployed in Italy

**RIGHT:** US soldiers ready mules for loading aboard landing craft for the landing in Sicily. Though the US Army was completely mechanised, mules were used to carry ammunition and rations in mountains.

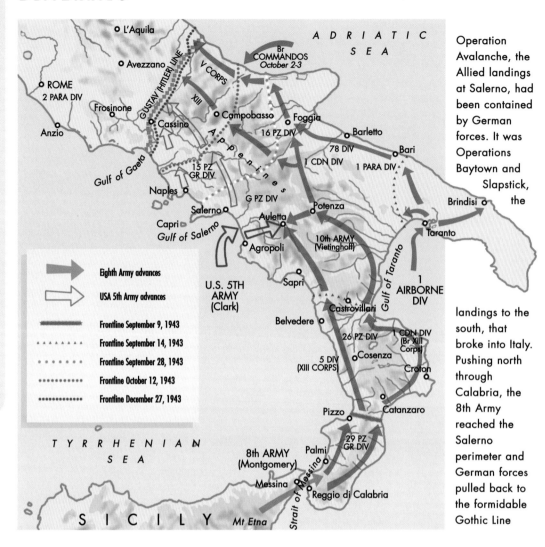

**ADRIATIC SEA**

L'Aquila

Avezzano

Br COMMANDOS
October 2-3

V CORPS

ROME
2 PARA DIV

Frosinone

XIII

Campobasso

Foggia

Cassino

16 PZ DIV

Barletto

Anzio

Bari

78 DIV
1 CDN DIV

1 PARA DIV

Gulf of Gaeta

15 PZ
GR DIV

Appenines

Naples

G PZ DIV

Potenza

Brindisi

Salerno

Capri
Gulf of Salerno

Auletta

Taranto

Agropoli

10th ARMY
(Vietinghoff)

Gulf of Taranto

1 AIRBORNE DIV

**Eighth Army advances**

**USA 5th Army advances**

Frontline September 9, 1943

Frontline September 14, 1943

Frontline September 28, 1943

Frontline October 12, 1943

Frontline December 27, 1943

U.S. 5TH ARMY
(Clark)

Sapri

Castrovillari

Belvedere

1 CDN DIV
(Br XIII Corps)

26 PZ DIV

5 DIV
(XIII CORPS)

Cosenza

Croton

TYRRHENIAN SEA

Pizzo

Catanzaro

8th ARMY
(Montgomery)

Palmi

29 PZ
GR DIV

Messina

Strait of Messina

Reggio di Calabria

SICILY

Mt Etna

Operation Avalanche, the Allied landings at Salerno, had been contained by German forces. It was Operations Baytown and Slapstick, the landings to the south, that broke into Italy. Pushing north through Calabria, the 8th Army reached the Salerno perimeter and German forces pulled back to the formidable Gothic Line

A USAAF Curtiss P-40 Warhawk flies over Mt Etna on Sicily.

The superb North American P-51D Mustang that provided long-range escorts for USAAF bombers.

## PARTY JOKES

The SD monitoring domestic morale in Germany reported on August 16, 1943 that "the people at present feel their powers of emotional resistance are being strained to the breaking point...Those wearing (Nazi) Party insignia have frequently been addressed by other Germans who say: 'What, are you still wearing that thing?'

"There have also been numerous reports of the following joke:

"Anyone who recruits five new members into the Party gets to leave himself. Anyone who recruits ten new members gets a certificate testifying that he was never in the Party."

came on May 20, 1943 when airfields in Sicily and Sardinia were attacked. In 48 hours at least 186 Axis aircraft were destroyed. The most spectacular attack was against Grosseto airfield, 144km (90 miles) north of Rome, where USAAF B-17 Flying Fortresses attacked leaving buildings wrecked and 58 Italian aircraft destroyed.

On May 28, 1943 the 2nd Special Air Service (SAS) Regiment undertook Operation Snapdragon, the reconnaissance of the fortified island of Pantalleria. The *Duce*, Benito Mussolini, had boasted that the tiny 51.5sq km (32sq mile) heavily fortified island would be a second Malta, resisting the Allied landings. The team which had been landed by subma-

**ABOVE:** A soldier of the Italian 184th Nembo Parachute Division. Italian troops would fight alongside the Germans on Sicily before siding with the Allies.

**LEFT:** A dust-covered Field Marshal Kesselring during a visit to the *Afrika Korps*. This *Luftwaffe* officer would fight a skilled ground campaign in Italy.

**ABOVE:** British and American soldiers are marched into captivity. Though the Allies were on the offensive, local counter attacks could yield prisoners.

**RIGHT:** A knocked out M4 Sherman lies on its side, possibly after being bulldozed off the road to free up traffic movement.

rine suffered no casualties but gained little information. In 100 hours the Allied air forces flew 5,000 sorties against it and dropped 6,096,000kg (6,000 tons) of bombs. It was then bombarded from the sea before the island's garrison surrendered to a sea-borne assault by the British 1st Div on June 11.

A day later the tiny Italian island of Lampedusa was bombarded from the air and sea. When Sergeant Jack Cohen, an RAF fighter pilot, developed engine trouble and was obliged to force land on the island, the garrison rushed out with white flags shouting "Can't you stop this?" He could not, and along with the garrison, sheltered for another two hours. Italian Army engineers on the island managed to repair his aircraft and he

**RIGHT:** In a gesture of Axis solidarity Italian *Alpini* mountain troops give Fascist salutes while German infantry applaud a speech in Sicily.

# SMART BOMBS

As part of the surrender agreement on September 10, 1943 the Italian fleet put to sea flying a black flag to be escorted to the Grand Harbour at Valetta, Malta and Gibraltar. The *Luftwaffe* reacted quickly, deploying a novel weapon against them, the guided glide bomb. It was the first "smart" bomb of the 20th century. There were two versions, the Ruhrstahl SD-1400 or Fritz X and the Henschel HS-293. Fritz X was basically a 1,400kg (3,100lb) armour-piercing bomb with fixed cruciform wings and a tail unit and radio guidance. Terminal velocity provided the impetus for this unpowered weapon. It scored its greatest success when three were launched and hit and sank the

Italian battleship *Roma* off Sardinia on its way to surrender. Other bombs damaged the British battleship HMS *Warspite* and the cruiser HMS *Uganda*. The Henschel HS-293 was a rocket-boosted glide bomb with a wingspan of 3.1m (10ft 3in) and a 500kg (1,100lb) warhead. It was powered by a Walter rocket that fired for 10 seconds and accelerated the bomb to 600km-h (375mph). A bright flare in the tail assisted the operator aboard the launch aircraft guide the bomb onto its target. The HS-293 became the first airborne guided missile to sink a ship when on August 27, 1943 one hit the sloop HMS *Egret* off northern Spain and caused her magazine to explode.

flew off to tell the US and Royal Navies that the island wished to surrender.

The surrender of Linosa, Lampedusa and Pantelleria cleared the way for Operation Husky, the invasion of Sicily.

Sicily was defended by the Italian 6th Army, a force of about 230,000 men under General Guzzoni with his HQ at Enna. There were coastal batteries covering likely invasion beaches and airfields along the southern and eastern shore. In addition to the Italian garrison the island had part of the 15th *Panzer Grenadier Div* and the élite *Panzerdivision Hermann Göring*. The key to the island was the port of Messina on the straits between Sicily and the Italian mainland. Held by the German and Italians, it allowed the island to be reinforced or evacuated, in Allied hands it secured the island

and was a jumping off point for an attack on the Italian peninsula.

On the night of July 9-10, 1943 British and American airborne forces landed on Sicily. They were the advance guard for the US 7th Army and British 8th Army. Of the 137 gliders released some 69 landed in the sea, and though the amphibious invasion force managed to rescue some of the soldiers about

**RIGHT:** A US Army Jeep and M10 Tank Destroyer smashed by artillery fire. A liaison officer in the Jeep may have gone forward to confer with the crew of the M10.

**LEFT:** With a Browning 9mm automatic pistol at the ready, a British sergeant moves cautiously forward as he stalks a German sniper. The Browning was made by Inglis of Canada.

200 were drowned. The British 1st Airlanding Brigade was tasked with the capture of the Simeto Bridge north of the town of Primasole. The British troops landing by glider were widely scattered, but of the 12 that landed near the bridge, the troops on board managed to hold it, until they were forced to withdraw. The troops who forced them out were men of *Fallschirmjäger* Regiment 3 (FJR 3), the Machine Gun and Engineer Battalions and elements of FJR 4. They had flown from bases in southern France, via Italy to Sicily and jumped at Catania airport on July 12 as part of a rapid reinforcement for the island.

US airborne forces were also badly scattered and 2,781 men were spread over a 80km (50-mile) radius.

The Anglo-American amphibious landings by the 15th Army Group commanded by General Alexander were in the south east tip of Sicily. The US 7th Army commanded by Patton landed at Licata and the US II Corps under General Omar Bradley between Gela and Scoglitte. Here they were faced respectively by the Italian 207 Coastal Div and 18 Coastal Brigade. (For details of Bradley's career see Blitzkrieg 7.)

**LEFT:** An M4 Sherman passes a knocked out PzKpfw IV fitted with *Schürzen* armour plates protecting the tracks and turret against shaped charge weapons.

**RIGHT:** A surprisingly accurate map of the Allied assault on Sicily published in *Signal*. It illustrates the way that German and Italian forces conducted a fighting withdrawal, pulling back towards Messina, and then effected an evacuation to the mainland.

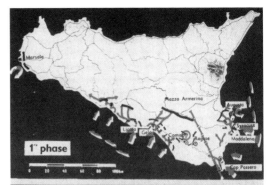

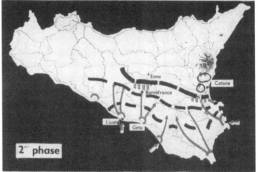

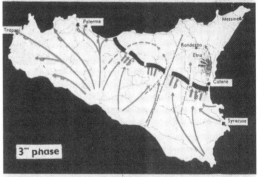

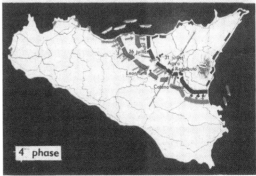

On July 11- 12 tanks of the *Panzerdivision Hermann Göring* launched a counter attack against the American 1st Infantry Div at Gela which had actually reached the coastal dunes before it was broken up by naval gunfire. It is estimated that over 5,000 naval shells rained down on the 60 tanks of *Panzerregiment Hermann Göring,* knocking out 40 PzKpfw III and IV tanks and 17 tanks of the Army *Tiger-Kompanie 2/504.*

The British 8th Army under Montgomery, composed of the XXX Corps under General Oliver Leese and the XIII under General Miles Dempsey, landed respectively at Pachino and between Avola and Cassible. They were faced by the Italian 204 Coastal Division.

**ABOVE:** A Messerschmitt Bf109 fighter in its dispersal bay that provides protection for the aircraft and any ground crew against air attack.

Kesselring moved the XIV Panzer Corps onto the island to bolster the Italian garrison. As the Allies piled on the pressure following their landings, Kesselring did not wait for clearance from Hitler before he began to withdraw his forces across the Straits of Messina into mainland Italy.

On July 29 the German press saluted Mussolini on his 60th birthday, which demonstrated Hitler's loyalty to his Fascist ally.

The German forces put up a strong resistance and their demolitions and rearguard actions meant that Messina did not fall until

**ABOVE AND LEFT:** The PzKpfw V Ausf D Panther that suffered from mechanical problems and lacked a hull machine gun. This was rectified in later marks and the tank, with its powerful 7.5cm Kw.K 42 gun, proved a formidable opponent both in Italy, North West Europe and the Eastern Front.

August 17, 1943. Its capture had become a race between the British under Montgomery and the US Army under Patton, both very competent but also men with huge personal egos. The Germans realised that Messina was critical and fought hard against the British 8th Army. At 10.15 the US 3rd Division entered Messina – Patton and the Americans had won by 50 minutes. Prior to the capture of Messina, in six days in Operation Lehrgang the German and Italian naval forces had evacuated 40,000 Germans, 60,0000 Italian troops, nearly 10,000 German vehicles and 47 tanks across the straits to the Italian mainland.

The cost of the Sicilian campaign had been

high. The British and Canadians had lost 2,721 killed, 2,183 missing and 7,939 wounded. The Americans had suffered 2,811 killed, 686 missing and 6,471 wounded. Axis losses were estimated at 164,000 killed or captured.

Secret negotiations between the Allies and Italy had confirmed that the Italians wanted to surrender and planned to arrest Mussolini in July. On September 3 the 8th Army crossed the Straits of Messina in Operation Baytown. On September 9, hours before the Italians announced their surrender, the British 1st Airborne Div landed at Brindisi.

In Operation Avalanche commanded by General Clark the US VIth Corps under Maj General Ernest Dawley and British X Corps under Lt General McCreery, with Commandos and Rangers, landed at Salerno. As a jumping off point for the capture of the city of Naples it was only 64km (40 miles) to the south. With Italy's withdrawal from the war they assumed that the landings would be unopposed.

The German 10th Army under General Heinrich von Vietinghoff had made an assessment of likely beachheads and reacted quickly to the Salerno landings. The 16th *Panzer* Division and 29th *Panzergrenadier* Division attacked the beach head and, supported by the *Luftwaffe*, put the Anglo-American force under such pressure that on September 14, when the Germans put in a particularly intense attack, there was some

**ABOVE:** The crew of a Junkers Ju188E-1 bomber are briefed for a night mission.

**LEFT:** A joint British RMP, US Military Police and Italian Carabinieri patrol in Naples following its liberation.

consideration about evacuating the coastal position. Clark ordered all men who could carry a rifle to man the front line as it was pushed back 3.2km (two miles). Naval gunfire and the deployment of the Mediterranean strategic airforce proved critical in defeating the German assaults. Two battalions of the 82nd Airborne Division under General Matthew Ridgeway were dropped on the cramped beachhead and 1,500 troops were transported by three cruisers from Tripoli.

In the end the XIII Corps of the 8th Army and the 1st Airborne Division advancing from the south forced the Germans to retire northwards to the Gustav Line. On September 10

German troops occupied Rome and five days later the 5th Army at the Salerno beachhead linked up with the 8th Army near Vallo di Lucania.

Clark's experience at Salerno would colour his advice to General John Lucas prior to his landing at Anzio.

On October 1, 1943, following a rising on September 27, Naples became the first major city in mainland Europe to be liberated. The cost of the campaign in southern Italy had been 12,000 British and US casualties. The city had been wrecked by systematic demolitions by the Germans. The harbour was choked with sunken ships and cranes. In the city there was a stink of raw sewage since the drainage system had been demolished along with the water supply.

Mussolini who on July 25 had been ordered to resign as leader of Italy by King Victor Emmanuel III, the Fascist Grand Council and Marshal Pietro Badoglio were arrested and held in a secret location. The king had told Mussolini the grim truth: "My dear *Duce*...my soldiers don't want to fight any more...at this moment, you are the most hated man in Italy."

By ingenious signals intercepts the Germans were able to find his prison, Campo Imperiale, a remote winter sports hotel in the Gran Sasso area of the Apennines. Since the hotel was at 2,100 metres (7,000 feet) and could only be reached by a funicular railway, an airborne assault was the only viable rescue option. On September 12, 1943 108 paratroops of the 1st Company of the *Fallschirmjäger Lehrbataillon* commanded by Lt. von Berlepsch and 26 *Waffen-SS* men commanded by *Obersturmbannführer* Otto Skorzeny lifted off in 12 DFS 230 gliders. (For specifications of the DFS 230 see *Blitzkrieg 2*.)

Eight of the gliders reached the rocky landing zone by the hotel and with no casualties Mussolini was rescued. Skorzeny

## OBERSTURMBANNFÜHRER OTTO SKORZENY

Born in Vienna on June 12, 1908 Otto Skorzeny was a striking figure nearly two metres (6.56 ft) tall. He trained as an engineer, then joined the Freikorps and the NSDAP in 1930. In the years before the war he worked as the business manager for a building contractor. In 1939 he joined the *Leibstandarte-SS "Adolf Hitler"* in 1940 he joined the *Waffen-SS Division "Das Reich"* and served on the Eastern Front. On September 12, 1943 he led the glider-borne raid on the hotel *Gran Sasso d'Italia* in the Abruzzi Apennines where Mussolini was being held by Italian forces and rescued him. He assisted in putting down the attempt to seize Berlin following the July Plot of 1944. In October 1944 he led a raid to kidnap the son of the Hungarian Regent Admiral Miklós Horthy and in this way Germany was able to pressurise the Hungarians to stay in the war up to 1945. In December 1944, in Operation Greif, he commanded a force of English-speaking German soldiers who penetrated American lines in US Army uniforms as part of the Ardennes Offensive. Many of these men were caught and subsequently shot. After the war Skorzeny was tried by an American military court and acquitted. He fled from an internment camp in Darmstadt in 1948 and, based in Spain and Ireland, worked to assist former *Waffen-SS* members escape from Germany. He died in Madrid on July 5, 1975.

**ABOVE AND RIGHT:** Otto Skorzeny lionised in a special issue of *Signal*.

**ABOVE AND LEFT:** Dressed in a black homburg hat and dark overcoat, Mussolini, accompanied by Otto Skorzeny, makes his way to the Fïesler Fi156c *Storch* liaison aircraft. The paratroops and *Waffen*-SS soldiers held the aircraft by its tail with its engine running until its engine had reached enough revolutions to allow it to take off.

greeted Mussolini with a cry of: "*Duce*, the *Führer* has sent me. You are free!" and the deposed Italian leader replied: "I knew my friend Adolf Hitler would not leave me in the lurch." Paratroops had seized the funicular railway, but Skorzeny and the Duce made their exit in a hazardous flight in a Fieseler *Storch* observation and liaison aircraft that took off from an improvised landing strip close to the hotel.

On September 13 Mussolini was reunited with his wife and Hitler in Bavaria and on September 25 he declared a new Italian Socialist Republic at Gargnano on Lake Garda in northern Italy. (For details of Mussolini's career see Blitzkrieg 4.)

# AEGEAN VICTORY

*I had fought in Russia and had always been told that in this war the British troops were poor fighters, but I never want to meet the British in a fight again. I had a belly full in Leros and would rather fight the Russians anyday.*

*German Company Commander PoW at Samos*
*November 1943*

Following the withdrawal of Italy from the Axis alliance, on September 12 1943 the British attempted to establish their presence in the southern Aegean with landings on the Italian-held Dodecanese islands of Kos, Samos and Leros off the Turkish coast.

For the British Prime Minister Winston Churchill operations in the Dodecanese were part of a larger plan in which the island of Rhodes would be attacked and occupied. The island had a reported garrison of 35,000 Italians and 7,000 Germans and if, with British assistance, the Italians attacked the Germans the operation would enjoy a high possibility of success. As a jumping off point for the attack Kos, Leros and Samos would be occupied.

The British felt that military success in the

Dodecanese would bring neutral Turkey into the war on the side of the Allies. This would not only reinforce the Allied forces in the eastern Mediterranean, but would also deny the German intelligence service, – the *Sicherheitsdienst* – access via Turkey to the USSR, a route they used to pass agents into the Caucasus. The SD ensured that the arrangement with Turkey remained amicable by passing on any intelligence that had been collected that might be of value to the Turks.

The Americans were unenthusiastic about the operation that they saw as a distraction from the main effort of the attack on Italy, and so the airpower available to support it would be strictly rationed. Interestingly, the OKW later had reservations about the feasibility of holding the Dodecanese and proposed a partial withdrawal from the area; Hitler vetoed this in orders issued on October 1, 1943.

The first British attack was an air raid by Liberator bombers on the airfields on Rhodes on September 13, 1943. Earlier, on September 8, Major Earl Jellicoe, Major Dolbey, an interpreter and a signaller from the Special Boat Squadron (SBS) had landed and contacted the Italian garrison. The commander of the Italian garrison, Admiral Campioni, made them welcome but would not commit himself to the Allies by attacking the Germans or simply holding out until the British arrived.

On September 14th the British did arrive, in the shape of the SBS who landed from *caiques* (Greek fishing boats) on Kos. The island that is 1.8km (1.11 miles) from Turkey is about 50km (31 miles) from east to west and 11km (6.8 miles) north to south. Its highest

**LEFT:** Knocked out and abandoned, a British Universal Carrier blocks the road in an Italian town. The Universal or Bren Gun Carrier was a popular easy-to-steer vehicle that could negotiate rough terrain and tow anti-tank guns.

## DIE SICHERHEITSDIENST

The *Sicherheitsdienst* SD (Security Service) the intelligence branch of the SS, was formed in March 1934 by Heinrich Himmler and included the *Sicherheitspolizei* – SIPO, Security Police, the *Kriminalpolizei* – KRIPO, the civilian criminal police service, the *Reichssicherheitshauptamt* – RSAH, Reich Central Security Office and even the *Schupos*, the ordinary city cops.

It was headed by Reinhard Heydrich who following his assassination in 1943 was succeeded by Ernst Kaltenbrunner. The SD devoted its energies to finding enemies of the state and under Heydrich chosen lawyers were quick to give a legal gloss to the arbitrary acts of the SD. The SD had its mix of thugs and highly intelligent operators like Walter Schellenberg.

Those who worked in the field seldom knew the identity of other members. The *Sicherheitsdienst* operating in Germany and Occupied Europe divided its contacts in the field into five classes. They were *Vertrauensleute* (V-men): Trusted Informants or confidants; *Agenten* (A-men): Agents; *Zubringer* (Z-men): Informants; *Helfershelfer* (H-men): Secondary Informants often with very dubious motives; and *Unzuverlässige* (U-men): those who were corrupt and had to be watched carefully. As the intelligence arm of the Nazi Party the SD was declared a criminal organisation at the Nuremberg Tribunals in 1945 and even honorary membership to be a crime.

point is a ridgeline about 935m (3,068 ft) high. On the north are a number of sandy beaches, but the south has a rocky coastline. There are two airfields at the towns of Marmari and Lambia.

After the SBS had completed its reconnaissance, Spitfires from No 7 Squadron South African Air Force arrived and during the night a company of 11th Bn The Parachute Rgt landed and joined the now co-belligerent Italian garrison of 5,000.

The 1st Bn the Durham Light Infantry (DLI) commanded by Lt Col R. F. Kirby began to arrive from Syria from the 18th by air, however by now Ju88s and Messerschmitt 109s were becoming a threat and attacked Dakotas and temporarily neutralised the main airfield with anti-personnel bombs. The DLI were unable to bring heavy weapons and equipment ashore because shipping was not available.

**BELOW:** A ferry carrying artillery, destined for the Dodecanese. The Germans achieved the critical concentration of force in time and space.

**RIGHT:** Fitted with drop tanks, Bf109 fighters on patrol. The *Luftwaffe* achieved air supremacy over the eastern Aegean because RAF aircraft were at the limit of their range.

## TRAITORS OR ALLIES

On October 13, 1943 Marshal Pietro Badoglio, the first premier of post Fascist Italy, had declared war on Germany and announced the formation of an Italian Army fighting alongside US and British forces in Italy. In his Order of the Day he told them: "You represent the true Italy. It is your destiny to liberate our country and drive the aggressor from our homeland. Show yourselves worthy of the great task that lies before you. We are proud of you." In a letter to General Eisenhower he wrote: "By this act, all ties with the dreadful past are broken, and my government will be proud to be able to march with you on to the inevitable victory."

To the Germans their former allies were now turncoats and traitors and many soldiers who were captured were shot. By late October a resistance organisation was beginning to grow within northern Italy, particularly as the Germans conscripted able-bodied men for forced labour. Where attacks were launched the Germans shot ten hostages for every German killed.

Badoglio had served with distinction in World War I, taking command after the disaster at Caporetto in 1917. He was put in charge after the failure of the Italian Army in its pre-war campaign in Ethiopia. He resigned in protest against Mussolini's plans to attack Greece in the winter of 1940.

# FALLSCHIRMJÄGERGEWEHR FG42

The *Luftwaffe* tasked Rheinmetall-Borsig with the mission of producing the *Fallschirmjägergewehr* FG 42. This weapon had a 20-round magazine, weighed 4.53kg and could fire at a cyclic rate of 750 to 800 rounds a minute. Interestingly, Rheinmetall, who designed the weapon, used the standard, and not the 7.92 *kurz* (short), rifle round which was used in the StG 43 and other assault rifles issued to the German Army.

There were two basic designs for the FG 42. One had a steel butt and sloping pistol grip and the other a wooden but and conventional grip. The weapon was in effect a light machine gun. It had a light bipod, flash eliminator and fixed folding bayonet. The FG 42 was capable of firing from a closed bolt for semi-automatic fire and from an open bolt for automatic fire. Though it

was an innovative weapon, it was also very expensive to produce and only 7,000 were made. In the late 1950s some of its design features were incorporated into the US M60 machine gun.

**ABOVE:** Only light *Kriegsmarine* ships were able to deploy in the Mediterranean, so U-Boats made the hazardous trip through the Straits of Gibraltar.

**ABOVE:** Germans soldiers disembark from pneumatic assault boats, having paddled from ships offshore during the landings on Kos on October 3, 1943.

Leros is an island about 15km (9.3 miles) long with two bays on the west coast and one, Alinda Bay, on the east where the capital Leros is located. The key to the island is Rachi Ridge, high ground between Alinda Bay and Gurna Bay on the east. The island is about 7 km (4.35 miles) wide at its widest point and has a central spine of hills reaching up to 180m (590.6ft).

On the island the Italians had built 24 naval batteries with a total of 100 guns of different calibres – however most of these were in open gun pits. The garrison consisted of 5,500 men, half of whom were administrative staff. There was only one infantry battalion of 1,000 men with obsolescent weapons and equipment.

The British deployed three battalions on Leros, the 4th Bn Royal West Kents (Buffs), 2nd Bn Royal Irish Fusiliers (RIF) and 1st Bn Kings Own Royal Rgt (KORR). In support was a troop of 25 Pounders — they were in fact

guns that had been captured by the Germans earlier in the war and fitted with German sights and ranging aids. Twelve 40mm Bofors guns of the 3rd Light AA Battery Royal Artillery (RA) provided air defence. They had rejected the idea of committing parachute troops because they thought the island was too rocky, in this assessment they were partly right.

Urged by Hitler to counter these moves, the Germans withdrew aircraft from southern France, Italy, Corsica and even southern Russia. By October 1 they had 362 aircraft in theatre consisting of 90 Ju88s and He111s, 50 Bf109s and 65 Ju87s. The Allies attempted to stop this build up with air attacks on airfields in Crete, Rhodes and Greece by Liberator, Halifax, Wellington and Hudson bombers of No 240 Wing and No 21 Group. The British were at a disadvantage because the ranges of 563.3km (350 miles) that aircraft and ships

**ABOVE:** In close formation the tough and reliable Ju52 transport aircraft carry paratroops and supplies to the islands of the Dodecanese.

had to operate at, meant that they had limited fuel for operations in the Dodecanese. The anti-aircraft defences on Kos, now strengthened by 40mm Bofors guns, were unable to prevent the *Luftwaffe* from neutralising the airfields and island-based fighters. The local superiority of the *Luftwaffe* meant that the Royal Navy could only operate in the area at night which gave them little opportunity for intercepting the German invasion convoys moving towards Kos.

The first German landings on Kos began at dawn on October 3. Some 1,200 troops commanded by Lt Gen Müller landed under cover of a massive air bombardment at Marmari. An Italian 75mm artillery battery opened fire against them and a platoon of the

**ABOVE:** A wounded British prisoner glances up at the photographer as a German soldier guards him in the cover of a ditch. A German patrol moves off down the road.

DLI went forward to investigate. The Germans also landed in the south of the island and at Camare Bay forced an Italian battery back into the hills. At Antimachia a company of paratroops from 1Bn FJR 2 landed and despite suffering casualties from small arms fire and the harsh terrain was able to establish a lodgement. The Germans were well supported by the *Luftwaffe* and had been able to land light artillery and armoured cars. The Germans broke up the Allied defenders into smaller groups and Colonel L.R.F. Kenyon, the garrison commander, decided that the British troops should attempt to escape into the hills and continue resistance as guerrillas. The withdrawal was covered by small groups, like the DLI Mortar Platoon that fought until it was overwhelmed. Some 105 troops were evacuated with the assistance of the SBS, however, 900 Allied troops and 3,000 Italians surrendered. Many Italians had taken no part in the fighting on either side, but despite this, 90 officers were executed by the SS.

There was now a pause and Allied planners realised that though it made strategic sense to evacuate Leros, the cost in shipping and aircraft might be very high. As the Germans regrouped for the attack, a troop-carrying convoy was intercepted on October 6 by the Royal Navy, probably on the basis of ULTRA decrypts, and 400 men and a battalion's worth of equipment were lost.

**ABOVE:** A German 21cm Mrs 18 howitzer dismantled for transport aboard a *Siebel* ferry. The modest freeboard made it essential that there was no swell if they were carrying cargo.

The garrison, commanded by the recently promoted Major-General F. Brittorous, would effectively have to hang on and hope for the best if attacked. He sited The Buffs with C Coy KORR in the north, 2 RIF with B Coy Royal West Kent Rgt in the centre and 1 KORR in the south. Mobility on the island was a problem both because of a lack of vehicles but also because the roads were very narrow and poor.

In his dispositions Brittorous attempted to cover all the possible beaches that could be used for landings. He discounted the possibility of an airborne assault despite the misgivings of Lt-Col Maurice French commanding the RIF.

**LEFT:** German infantry work their way forward across rugged terrain. The *Fallschirmjäger* dropped from Ju52s at low altitude on wind-swept rocky DZs, so suffered many injuries.

**ABOVE:** British soldiers captured on Kos are marched into captivity. Not until Arnhem in September 1944 would the British suffer such a comprehensive defeat.

The anticipated attack came at about 04.30 on November 12 with a convoy making for Palma, Grifo and Pendelli Bays. Italian coastal batteries and British 25 Pounders and Bofors guns opened fire and six German landing craft were sunk. In the north at Palma the Germans were thrown back by a counter attack by D Coy The Buffs. However, at Grifo Bay, two companies landed and moved rapidly inland. They seized the rugged heights of Mount Clidi, destroyed the Italian coastal battery near its summit and dug in. Subsequent British counter attacks failed to dislodge them.

During the afternoon of November 12 12 waves of Ju52 transports flew in and dropped 500 men of 1Bn FJR 2 on the narrow neck of land between Gurna and Alinda Bays. A combination of strong winds and accurate fire from SBS and other Special Forces detachments as well the RIF and Royal West Kents caused 60% casualties, but under cover of *Luftwaffe* strikes the survivors dug in. They had effectively split the island and seized Rachi Ridge.

The Germans and British fought a succession of actions to capture or recapture dominant features on the island. In the second major British counter attack on the 15th, the Germans holding the Appetici feature and Rachi Ridge were seriously pressed, so General Müller considered evacuating the island. The British attack was ill co-ordinated and not in sufficient strength, and daylight *Luftwaffe* ground support saved the day for the Germans flying between 400 and 500 sorties. In this action the gallant Colonel

French was killed leading his battalion.

At 17.30 on the 16th with the Germans now controlling key areas of the island the British garrison commander formally surrendered. The Italians, whom the Germans now called "guerrilla partisans", surrendered at 18.30.

For the Germans victory in the Dodecanese was a major propaganda coup and with the exception of Arnhem in 1944 would be the last time they took British prisoners in any numbers.

Samos was evacuated by the SBS during the night of November 19-20.

British and Greek naval losses were six destroyers, two submarines and ten coastal craft sunk; the RAF lost 115 aircraft; and army casualties amounted to 4,800, most of whom were captured.

The German losses were 12 merchant ships and 20 landing craft sunk and 4,000 casualties of whom the bulk were drowned.

**ABOVE:** British, Indian and Italian PoWs await evacuation from Port Laki, Leros, with the German destroyer TA-16 tied up in the background.

**BELOW:** General F. Müller (left) confers with Brigadier Tilney followed the British surrender on Leros. An officer interpreter stands between them.

# THE GUSTAV LINE

*It is not sufficient to give clear and tactically correct orders. All officers and men of the Army, the Air Force and the Naval forces must be penetrated by a fanatical will to end the battle victoriously, and never to relax until the last enemy soldier has been destroyed or thrown back into the sea. The battle must be fought in a spirit of holy hatred.*

*Teleprinter signal from Adolf Hitler to Field Marshal Kesselring,*

In Italy the Germans withdrew to the Gustav, or Winter, Line that had been built in the Apennines, running from the mouth of the Garigliano, through Monte Cassino to a point south of Ortona. The line was held for by 15 divisions of the German 10th Army. The battle for the Gustav Line and its key position, the sixth-century mountain-top Benedictine monastery of Monte Cassino, became an epic of endurance by the German paratroopers, *Fallschirmjäger*, who held the position.

**ABOVE:** *Fallschirmjäger* shelter in an Italian farm. They would prove formidable opponents for the Allies.

On October 9 the 5th Army closed on the River Volturno but skilful German demolitions and the rain delayed the US forces who were unable to advance until October 24. Between November 5 and 14, troops of the British 56th and US 3rd Infantry Divisions closed up to the Bernhard Line in front of the Gustav Line and fought a tough battle to seize Monte Camino that dominated the River Garigliano. On the eastern side of the Italian peninsula the 8th Army under Montgomery had reached the River Sangro on November 8.

On November 15 Alexander ordered Clark to halt his attacks south of the Garigliano. The men of the 5th Army were exhausted and had suffered heavy casualties. Five days later the 8th Army crossed the Sangro and on November 28 began the assault on the Gustav Line. Though the V Corps overran it at its eastern end, casualties mounted and the advance slowed.

On December 2 Clark resumed his attacks and in four days' heavy fighting the British 56th Division captured Monte Camino, and

## GENERAL MARK W. CLARK

Mark Wayne Clark was born in Madison Barracks, New York, in 1896. At 17, with the assistance of his aunt, Zettie Marshall (the mother of General George C. Marshall), Clark secured an early appointment to the U.S. Military Academy. A tall, lean, and often sickly youth, Clark failed to distinguish himself at West Point as either an athlete or scholar, graduating 110th in a class of 139 in 1917. He was able to cultivate friendships with officers who would rise to high rank in the US Army and this helped to further his career.

Between 1942 and 1945 he served in World War II as Deputy Commander in Chief of the Allied forces invading North Africa, and commanded the US 5th Army during the invasion of Italy. He was US High Commissioner for Austria from 1945 until 1947. Returning to the United States, he commanded the 6th Army from 1947 until 1949 and was Chief of the Army Field Forces from 1949 until 1952. He was Supreme Commander of the United Nations forces in the Korean War during 1952 and 1953. Clark was President of the

Citadel Military Academy in Charleston, South Carolina, from 1954 until 1966. He died in 1984.

**ABOVE:** With moments to go before they move out on another fighting patrol, *Fallschirmjäger* stow *Stielgranate* – stick grenades – in their belts. The stick grenade had a four-second delay fuze.

**RIGHT:** A mule convoy carries rations and ammunition to French troops high in the mountains.

two days later the US II Corps seized Monte la Difensa and Monte Maggiore. Opposite them the German 10th Army withdrew to the Gustav Line. From December 6 to December 17 the US 143rd Infantry Regiment fought to drive German forces from the Italian town of San Pietro. Some 100 *Panzergrenadiere* caused 1,500 US casualties. It was a pointer of what was to come in street fighting in Italy.

Two days after Christmas the 1st Canadian

**LEFT:** Captured German *Fallschirmjägen*, some walking wounded, bring in a British soldier who has lost a foot on an anti-personnel mine. Mines restricted movement for vehicles and men, and non-lethal, but crippling, injuries to soldiers sapped morale and made men cautious.

**BELOW LEFT:** General Alexander confers with the tough US General Lucian "Old Gravel Guts" Truscott. Truscott would be a bold and imaginative commander at Anzio.

Division captured Ortona after fierce house to house fighting. It had been prepared for defence with considerable ingenuity with bunkers onto which buildings had been deliberately demolished for added protection

## ANZIO ANNIE

A huge 41.23m (135.28ft) long 283mm (11.14in) calibre German rail gun would emerge from a tunnel overlooking the Anzio beachhead and subject British and US forces to unexpected barrages. The Allied soldiers named it "Anzio Annie", but in fact it was one of a mark of rail gun developed by the Germans designated 28cm K5E or M42 and informally known as Bertha Schlanke, Léopold and Bruno. Two examples survive, one at the Atlantic Wall Museum in France and the other at the Aberdeen Proving Grounds in the United States. In action the gun weighed 218,000kg (214.59 tons) and, firing a 255kgh (662lb) shell, had a muzzle velocity of 1120m/s (3,700fps) and a range of 62.4km (38.6 miles). The 21.5m (70ft) barrel elevated from 0° to 50° and traversed 2°.

**ABOVE:** A *Fallschirmjäger* MG42 machine gun crew hunker low in the ruins of one of the buildings in Monte Cassino town. The MG42 had a cyclic rate of 1,550rpm.

**RIGHT:** The Abbot of the Benedictine Monastery of Monte Cassino, Georgio Diamere, is assisted from a German staff car by General von Senger und Etterlin.

# MONTE CASSINO

Monte Cassino, Benedictine monastery, situated on the hill of the same name overlooking the town of Cassino, Italy, north-west of Naples, was founded in 529 by St Benedict of Nursia on the site of an Apollonian temple. It became the home of

the Benedictine Order and was for many centuries the leading monastery in western Europe. It was destroyed by Lombards in 590, by Saracens in 884, and by earthquake in 1349, and rebuilt each time. The present buildings are in the style of the 16th and 17th centuries. During the 11th and 12th centuries it was a centre of learning, particularly in the field of medicine. The famous medical school at Salerno was established by Monte Cassino monks. In 1866, when monasticism was abolished in Italy, Monte Cassino was made a national monument. In pre-war staff exercises Italian officers had identified Monte Cassino and the surrounding mountains as the key defensive area to block an approach to Rome from the south. The Germans were quick to realise this as well in 1943.

## GENERAL EBERHARD VON MACKENSEN

**ABOVE:** An up-armoured German 7.5cm *StuG* III assault gun manoeuvres across a narrow Italian bridge. Assault guns proved very effective defensive weapons.

Born in 1889, the son of the Field Marshal August von Mackensen, Eberhard entered his father's old cavalry regiment, the Death's Head Hussars, and served with distinction in World War I. In World War II he commanded a tank corps and later the 1st Panzer Army on the Eastern Front. As a Colonel General he commanded the 14th Army that held the Allies at the beachhead at Anzio in 1944. After the war he was found guilty of shooting hostages and sentenced to life imprisonment but was released in 1952. He died in 1969.

and concealment. Heavy casualties and the onset of winter slowed the advance of the 8th Army.

Montgomery relinquished command of the 8th Army to General Sir Oliver Leese on January 8 and returned to Great Britain to join the senior command group for Operation Overlord.

On January 17 the 5th Army attacked across the Garigliano and the British X Corps commanded by General Richard McCreery established bridgeheads. The US II Corps attacked on January 20 and the US 34th Infantry Division succeeded in getting across the Rapido but was halted below Monte

**LEFT:** Bearded and exhausted, German paratroopers scan Allied positions from a forward OP.

**BELOW:** A *StuG* III commander uses the protection and cover of a ruined building in Monte Cassino.

**BELOW:** British prisoners assist a wounded comrade as they are evacuated from the fighting. The Geneva Conventions laid down strict rules about the treatment of captured and wounded enemy soldiers.

**ABOVE:** A German patrol sprints through the jumble of masonry and fallen timber – areas like this concealed snipers and mines and were a deadly battleground for German and Allied troops.

**ABOVE:** A *Fallschirmjäger* in the distinctive splinter-pattern camouflaged smock crawls forward to observe. He has used a loop of rubber inner tube as a helmet band and fixed grass to break up the outline of his helmet.

**ABOVE:** A diagrammatic map that appeared in *Signal,* the German propaganda magazine. Key lines and features are numbered. They include 1) Cassino town; 2) Castle Hill; 3) The Monastery; 5) The Rapido; 6) and 7) German lines and attacks; 8) Allied attempt to outflank the position; 11) and 12) Fighting in Monte Cassino town and attempts to cross the Rapido; 13) Landings at Anzio; 14) German counter attacks at Anzio; 15) Artillery fire on the Monastery.

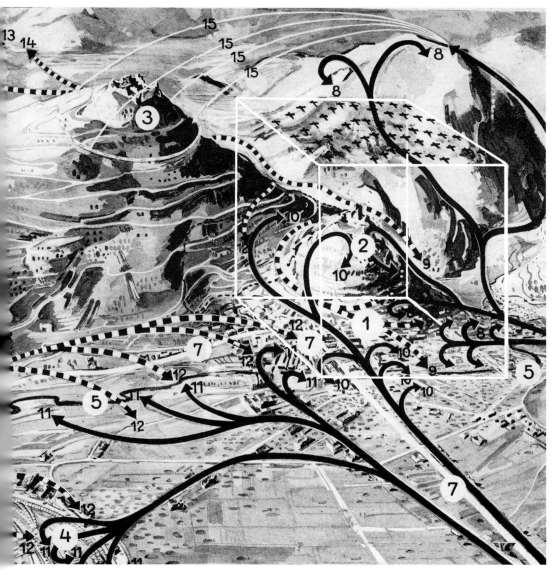

**FAR LEFT:** *Luftwaffe* General Heidrich, the commander of *Fallschirmjäger* Div 1, who took over from General Baade's 90th Panzer Grenadier Div at Cassino.

**LEFT:** Black smoke and earth geyser upwards as a stick of bombs lands on the outskirts of Cassino town. The ability of the paratroops to survive pounding by bombs and artillery and emerge to repel Allied attacks impressed Hitler.

**RIGHT:** A British HQ dug in on the front line of the Anzio perimeter. Veterans of World War I said that the grim conditions of mud, dirt and rain at Anzio were similar to the Western Front. British and American troops were pressed hard by German counter attacks.

**BELOW:** Paratroops carry a wounded comrade through a wrecked Italian city. Evacuating men wounded in street fighting was extremely difficult since ambulance vehicles could not move through streets clogged with rubble.

Cassino. The 36th Division was repulsed as it attempted to cross the swollen river and suffered heavy casualties.

The Anzio landings took place on January 22, but did not manage to unhinge the Gustav Line. Two days later the North African troops of the French Expeditionary Force attacked across the Rapido north of Monte Cassino but were stopped short of Monte Cassino by fierce German counter attacks.

On Tuesday February 15 at the urging of General Freyberg, the commanding general of the II New Zealand Corps fighting in central Italy, the USAAF attacked the monastery of Monte Cassino. In a daylight raid 142 B-17s, B-125s and B-26s dumped 436,900kg (453 tons) of bombs onto the buildings. The Allies were convinced that the Germans were at the least using the commanding position of the building for artillery observation posts and at worst had fortified it. Once the building had been reduced to ruins the paratroops moved in and fortified them. Their stubborn defence earned them a unique tribute from Hitler who asserted that they were harder than the

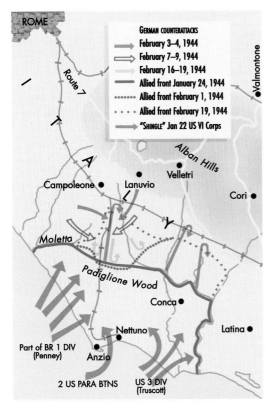

**ABOVE:** A DUKW on the sandy beach at Anzio. This versatile amphibious truck could carry stores from ships offshore to dumps inland.

**LEFT:** Operation Shingle, the landing at Anzio that achieved complete surprise and should have unhinged the German position at Cassino. Kesselring's quick reactions, however, as well as counter attacks nearly drove the US and British forces back into the sea. Like Salerno, the break out from the beachhead was only possible after friendly forces had closed with Anzio.

## DUKW

Developed from the GMC 6 x 6 chassis, the DUKW, universally known as the "Duck", was the brainchild of an American boat designer whose previous experience had been designing ocean racing yachts. The US Army was initially resistant to the concept of an amphibious truck, but the rescue of the crew of a Coast Guard cutter during a storm off the US coast convinced them of its utility. From 1942 it would become a key vehicle in the amphibious operations in Europe and the Far East and over 21,000 would be built before the end of the war.

| | |
|---|---|
| Armament: | n/a |
| Armour: | n/a |
| Crew: | 2 |
| Weight: | 9,097kg (6.64 tons) |
| Hull length: | 9.75m (37ft) |
| Width: | 2.51m (8ft 2in) |
| Height: | 2.69m (8ft 10in) |
| Engine: | GMC Model 270 91hp |
| Road speed: | 80km/h (50mph) |
| Water speed: | 9.7km/h (6mph) |
| Range: | 120km (75miles) |

**ABOVE:** Soldiers of the *Hermann Göring* Division lie dead in a drainage ditch in the Pontine Marshes following an abortive attack against US positions.

*Waffen-SS*. The New Zealanders and men of the 4th Infantry Division who attacked following the bombing were halted by savage German resistance.

The Germans made considerable propaganda mileage out of the destruction of the monastery and had taken the precaution of removing over 70,000 volumes and 1,2000 original documents to safety in the Vatican. The operation was undertaken by Lt Colonel Julius Schlegel of the *Hermann Göring Panzer* Division who, as an art lover, realised that the works were at risk. The Bishop and Abbot of Monte Cassino, Gregorius Diamare, presented Schlegel with a manuscript to express his gratitude and thanks. Allied propaganda suggested that Schlegel had looted the monastery and after the war Field Marshal Alexander intervened to endorse

**ABOVE:** A young soldier from the *Hermann Göring* Division hunched over his Kar 98K rifle in front of a rudimentary barbed wire obstacle. His cuff title can be seen on his tunic sleeve.

the monks of Cassino to assert that the art treasures had been saved and not stolen. However, elsewhere in Italy art treasures and buildings were vandalised or destroyed. Historical bridges were destroyed and the ruins mined to delay repair.

**ABOVE:** Exhausted and wounded British soldiers in a crude trench at Anzio. Though sandy soil was easy to dig, it was also poor protection from artillery fire.

**BELOW:** A picture of British soldiers, which although probably posed for propaganda purposes, captures the confusion and violence of the street fighting.

**RIGHT:** With the fighting over, a Staghound armoured car drives through Cassino town. In the background are the ruins on Castle Hill that were fought over fiercely by British and German forces.

## UNIVERSAL CARRIER

Widely known as the Bren Gun Carrier, the Carden-Loyd Universal carrier was developed in 1939 from the Carden-Loyd series of light tanks and reconnaissance vehicles. There were numerous marks of which only one was designed to carry the infantry section automatic weapon, the Bren gun.

Driving controls were identical to those of a truck, steering was by wheel, small movements bowed the track and sharper movements brought the steering bakes into play.

About 35,000 were built in the UK during World War II, manufacturers including Aveling-Barford, Ford, Sentinel, Thornycroft and Wolseley. Some 5,600 were built in Australia, 520 in New Zealand and over 29,000 in Canada. In the United States 14,000 were built as the T16. Production of the Universal Carrier ceased in 1945.

| | |
|---|---|
| Armament: | One Bren 7.7mm (0.303in) LMG, or one 12.7mm (.50in) Boys AT rifle |
| Armour: | 12mm (0.47in) |
| Crew: | 4 - 5 |
| Hull length: | 3.75m (12ft 4in) |
| | Width 2.10m (6ft 11in) |
| | Height 1.60m (5ft 3in) |
| Weight: | 4,318kg (4.25 tons) |
| Powerplant: | Ford 8-cylinder water-cooled inline petrol developing 63.3kW (85bhp) |
| at | 2,800rpm |
| Speed: | 51km/h (32mph) |
| Range: | 256km (160 miles) |

# M10 TANK DESTROYER

The Tank Destroyer or "TD" was lightly armed and had an open turret, but its powerful gun derived from an AA gun was a good tank killer. Based on the M4 Sherman chassis, the production run was only from September to December 1942, and nearly 5,000 were produced. The M10 was not deployed in separate tank destroyer battalions, as had been envisaged in the early 1940s, but as an assault weapon.

| | |
|---|---|
| Armament: | 1 76.2mm M7 gun; one 12.7mm Browning |
| Armour: | 12 to 37mm (0.47 to 1.46in) |
| Crew: | 5 |
| Weight: | 29.937kg (29.47 tons) |
| Hull length: | 6.83m (22ft 5in) |
| Width: | 3.05m (10ft) |
| Height: | 2.57m (8ft 5in) |
| Engine: | Two General Motors six-cylinder diesel engines developing 375hp |
| Road speed: | 51km/h (32mph) |
| Range: | 322km (200 miles) |

Almost a month later attacks by the 4th Indian Division and the New Zealand 6th Infantry Brigade were preceded by four hours of bombardment. Some 755 bombers attacked – two aircraft for every 350 German paratroopers or five tons of high explosive for each soldier. The air attacks were backed by an artillery bombardment in which 195,969 shells were fired into the town and defences of the monastery. Incredibly, the Germans hung on, though Gurkha soldiers achieved the deepest penetration, reaching the exposed position of Point 435 or "Hangman's Hill" only 402m (440yds) from the monastery. The Gurkhas, Essex Regiment and Rajput

Rifles were to hang on there under German fire, supplied only by night until they were finally evacuated on March 25.

The fighting had cost the 2nd New Zealand Division 63 officers and over 800 men killed, wounded or missing from an all-volunteer army drawn from a small island community. The 4th Indian Division had lost 1,000 men and 65 officers.

Kesselring's tactical genius was amply demonstrated when in Operation Shingle, an attempt to outflank the Gustav Line, the US VI Corps composed of the US 3rd and British 1st Infantry Divs landed on a 24.1km (15-mile) stretch of Italian beach near the pre-war resort towns of Anzio and Nettuno on January 22, 1944.

The area was defended by two battalions and the Allies under General John P. Lucas had achieved complete surprise. However, because of a lack of clarity in his orders and indicators from ULTRA that the Germans would counter attack, Lucas did not exploit his success and Kesselring set in motion Operation Richard, the contingency plan to counter an Allied amphibious attack and ordered the 14th Army into the area.

Churchill, an advocate of the operation, cabled Alexander: "Am glad you are pegging out claims rather than digging in." In fact, warned by Clark, who was aware of Operation Richard through ULTRA intercepts, "not to stick his neck out", Lucas set up his HQ in a wine cellar in the port and concentrated on building up his strength in the area.

On January 29 the VI Corps began to attack out of the Anzio beachhead. The 3rd Div advanced towards Cisterna and the 1st towards Albano in the Alban Hills but both

**ABOVE:** A bulldozer leads a convoy of US trucks off a causeway constructed for Landing Ship Tanks (LST) off the beach at Anzio.

**LEFT:** With the harbour at Anzio secured, US LSTs could dock and offload tanks directly. Here an M4 Sherman grinds ashore and inland.

**ABOVE:** US General Lucas who managed to land considerable forces and stores, but failed to exploit the surprise of the Anzio landings.

**BELOW:** Smoke rises from two US landing ships from Force X – one the victim of a mine and the other air attack.

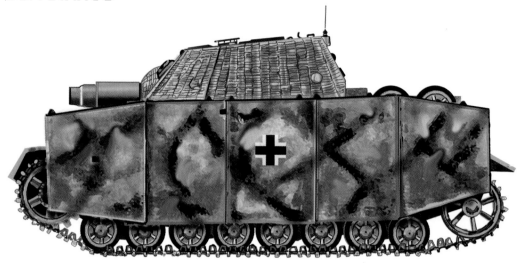

## STURMPANZER IV BRUMMBÄR

Between 1943-44 the Vomag factory at Plauen produced 313 StuPz43 or *Sturmpanzer IV Brummbär* – Growly Bear, or *Sturmhaubitze* 43L/12 auf Fgst PzKpfw IV (Sf) SdKfz166. This was a distinctively different vehicle with a high silhouette and a box-like fighting compartment. The main armament, the 15cm *Sturmhaubitze L/12*, was in a ball mounting and the vehicle carried 38 rounds. It used the PzKpfw IV F, G, H and J chassis. The sides were protected by Schürzen. The vehicle armour arrangement changed in later models consisting of two plates at the front instead of one. The Brummbär was first used in action at Kursk in 1943 and over 300 vehicles were produced by the *Deutsche Eisenweke*.

| | |
|---|---|
| Armament: | 15cm (5.91in) *Sturmhaubitze* 43 |
| Armour: | 10mm to 100mm (0.39in to 3.94in) |
| Crew: | 5 |
| Weight: | 28,650kg (28.2 tons) |
| Hull length: | 5.93m (19 ft 5in) |
| Width: | 2.88m (9ft 5in) |
| Height: | 2.52 m (8ft 3in) |
| Engine: | Maybach HL 120 TRM V-12 petrol, 300bhp |
| Road speed: | 40km/h (24mph) |
| Range: | 210km (130 miles) |

attacks were held by the German 14th Army. Two days later US Rangers waded 6.4km (4 miles) at night through flooded drainage ditches to attack the village of Cisterna but were detected at the last moment and only six men survived the fire from tanks and infantry.

On the night of January 29-30 the British 24 Guards Brigade attacked the village of Carroceto where the 29th *Panzergrenadier* Regiment was dug in and in the fighting suffered heavy casualties.

On February 3 the Germans counter attacked, hitting the British 1st Division and driving it back in nine days of savage fighting. The Germans were, however, exhausted and had suffered heavy casualties, and paused for four days.

On February 16 the I *Fallschirm* Corps under General Schlemm and the LXXVI Panzer Corps General Herr with total of ten divisions, among which was the élite *Panzerdivision Hermann Göring*, had been assembled around the "Anzio abscess" as Hitler called the besieged beachhead where five Allied divisions were trapped. Von Mackensen launched a fierce attack against the battered British sector. Yelling the battle cries of the victory years of World War II, infantry supported by tanks crashed into the

**LEFT:** Dressed in khaki drill tropical uniforms *Fallschirmjägen*, distinctive by their rimless helmets, watch from a forward OP. Following a sustained and heavy bombardment by 800 guns for six hours. *Fallschirmjäger* Division I earned the tribute from General Alexander: "I doubt whether there is another unit in the world that could endure that and continue fighting."

## REPUBLIC P-47D THUNDERBOLT

The Thunderbolt was the biggest and heaviest fighter ever to have served in the USAAF when it entered service in 1942. It was popular with its pilots, being well able to absorb battle damage and consequently suffering a very low loss rate. As the air war swung against the *Luftwaffe,* the Thunderbolt was used in the ground attack role and later in North West Europe against V1 missiles and Me163 and Me262 fighters. The blister canopy adopted from the British Hawker Typhoon soon replaced the sliding canopy that had earned the early P-47 the nickname "Razorback".

| | |
|---|---|
| Type: | Fighter/ fighter bomber |
| Crew: | 1 |
| Power Plant: | One 2,300hp Pratt & Whitney R-2800-21 or 2,535 hp R-2800-59 |
| Performance: | Maximum speed at 9,155m (30,000ft) 697km/h (433mph) Maximum range 1609km (1,000 miles) |
| Weights: | Empty 4,491kg (9,900lb) Maximum 6,804kg (15,000lb) |
| Dimensions: | Wing span 12.43m (40ft 9in) Length 11.01m (36ft 1in) Height 4.44m (14ft 7in) |
| Armament: | Six or eight .50in Browning machine guns; bomb racks with a maximum load of 1,134kg (2,500lb) or ten 5 in rocket projectiles. |

1st Division and there was a real danger that the beachhead would be split in two. Only the massive firepower of ships, artillery and bombers halted the attack at Carroceto Creek.

In North West Europe the operation was followed closely by the Germans since it was a testing ground for tactics that might be employed when the Allies launched the Second Front. An aggressive counter attack of the beach head that would be favoured by Rommel appeared to have failed.

On February 22 Lucas was replaced by the more combative General Lucian "Old Gravel Guts" Truscott as commander at Anzio. A week later he received a baptism of fire when the US 3rd Division came under attack by four divisions. Once again air power and artillery saved the Allies and on March 3 von Mackensen called a halt to attacks.

On May 23, following stalemate and siege, the US VI Corps broke out of the Anzio beachhead. German resistance was fierce but a day later the Allies cut Highway 7

**ABOVE:** With bayonets fixed on their SMLE rifles Polish soldiers make their way through the ruins of the monastery. The "sword" bayonet was an intimidating extension to the rifle, however very few men were killed by bayonets in the war.

**ABOVE AND LEFT:** Not long after capture, *Fallschirmjägen* prisoners are escorted to the lea of an M4 Sherman. Though disarmed they outnumber their New Zealand captors who have sensibly concentrated them in an area where the tank and hillside provide barriers on two sides. As the German paratroopers are assembled they look far from cowed and appear to be sizing up their chances of overwhelming their captors and making a break.

creating a wedge between the 10th and 14th Armies. On May 25 the US II and VI Corps linked up on Highway 7and this marked the end of the four months' isolation of the Anzio beachhead that had in places become similar to the trenches of World War I.

During the four months of the Anzio Campaign the Allied VI Corps suffered over 29,200 combat casualties (4,400 killed, 18,000 wounded, 6,800 prisoners or missing) and 37,000 noncombat casualties. Two-thirds of these losses, amounting to 17 percent of VI Corps' effective strength, were inflicted between the initial landings and the end of the German counteroffensive on March 4. German combat losses, suffered wholly by the 14th, were estimated at 27,500 (5,500 killed, 17,500 wounded, and 4,500 prisoners

# BLITZKRIEG

or missing) – figures very similar to Allied losses.

Among the German soldiers who died at Anzio was Alexander Paulus, the son of Field Marshal Paulus who had surrendered at Stalingrad a year earlier. (For details of Field Marshal Paulus see *Blitzkrieg* 5.)

The final battle for the Gustav Line, Operation Diadem on May 13, saw 2,000 guns bombarding the German positions backed by 3,000 aircraft. The Polish II Corps isolated the monastery as the British crossed the Liri river west of Cassino to cut Route 6 west of the town and the US and French Corps attacked south of the river. The tough French *Goumiers*, Moroccan mountain troops of General Juin's *Corps Expéditionaire Français,* took Monte Faito where the German 71st Division had followed orders and fought with no plan for withdrawal. The 8th Indian and 4th British crossed the fast flowing Rapido River where they hit well-sited bunkers and defences and the Poles attacked the monastery from the east and north.

On May 18 the Polish flag was hoisted over the ruins of the monastery of Monte Cassino. The Polish II Corps under General Wladyslaw Anders had been losing 30 men a day as it prepared for the assault and when it went in had lost a fifth of its strength. In the first 90 minutes of the final battle, communications broke down and the Poles were forced to withdraw. They went back and supported by 200 air strikes stormed into the ruined monastery.

The four-month battle for the Monte Cassino position had cost the Allies 21,000 casualties including 4,100 killed; German losses were comparable.

A combination of Kesselring's tactical skill and General Clark's ambition to see the US 5th Army liberate Rome allowed the German 10th Army to evade encirclement after the capture of Cassino. Ironically, Clark's moment of glory as he entered Rome would be fleeting. The city had been declared "Open" by Kesselring on June 4 and German troops ordered to withdraw and not to fight in the streets.

RIGHT: Following the fall of Rome the Germans continued to fight a successful withdrawal action through fortified lines constructed across the Italian mountains. The "Hitler Line" was renamed after they realised it might fall.

LEFT: A German machine gun crew in a well concealed position survey the ground covered by the fire from their MG42.

**LEFT:** As smoke rises from an Italian farmhouse hit by shell fire, a German patrol observes from dead ground below the lip of the hill.

Clark and the 5th Army entered on June 5 but a day later Operation Overlord, the Allied landings in Normandy, became the big story on radio and in the newspapers and Clark became yesterday's news.

The Germans meanwhile withdrew through a series of defensive switch lines including the Caesar Line, that for a short time was known as the Hitler Line. They were able to join other forces on the 16km (9.94-mile) deep Gothic Line that ran from La Spezia on the west to the Adriatic, between Pesaro and Cattolica. By June 16 they were consolidated in their new positions.

The fight for the Gothic Line would be the last major German defensive battle in Italy.

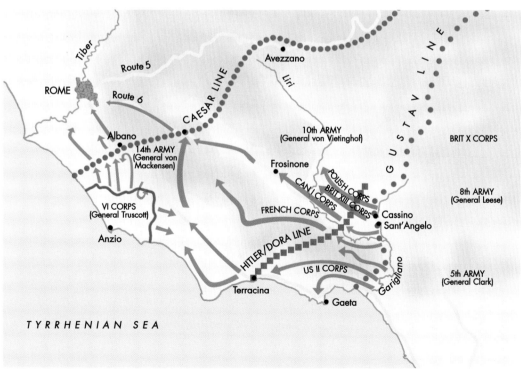

# THE ETERNAL CITY
# AND BEYOND

*The capture of Rome is a vast, world-wide event, and should not be minimised. I hope that British as well as Americans will enter the city simultaneously. I would not lump it in with other towns taken on the same day.*

*Winston Churchill to General Alexander*
*May 31, 1944*

In the dusty dawn of August 25, 1944 British, Canadian and Polish troops launched the first probing attacks on the Gothic Line – the German defences in Italy – based on the mountain chain of the Apennines, and to the east, the River Foglia and Pesaro. It was not until September 12 that the battle would begin in earnest.

Following the fall of Rome on June 4, 1944 the German forces in Italy fell back on the intermediate Albert Line that ran from Grosseto on the west, past Lake Trasimene to the river Chienti and to the Adriatic east coast.

As early as June 1, 1944 Kesselring had decided to make a stand on the line of the northern Apennines. He knew that he would need until autumn to prepare the positions, and so it was necessary to fight a series of delaying actions through the summer. Italy lent itself to defensive fighting, and the Germans fought a series of masterful withdrawals. The country was a narrow peninsula with steep mountains, narrow winding roads

**ABOVE LEFT:** With stick grenades along the parapet of his mountain look out, a *Fallschirmjäger* scans the terrain. If he saw suspicious movement he could call for artillery or mortar fire.

**LEFT:** Paratroopers firing a Kurzer 8cm *Granatwerfer*, a cut down 81mm mortar, used by *Fallschirmjäger* and special units. It had a maximum range of 1,100m (1,203yd) with a 3.5kg (7.72lb) bomb.

**FAR LEFT:** A 2cm *Gebirgsflak* gun crewed by German mountain troops – *Gebirgsjäger*. The gun carriage was too light for long bursts where vibration made the gun inaccurate.

# BLITZKRIEG

**BELOW:** After the fall of Rome the Germans withdrew in good order to a prepared position known as the Gothic Line. They delayed the Allied advance with demolitions, mines and by holding switch lines – temporary defensive positions.

Legend:

- Allied forces push towards the Gothic Line
- Gothic Line
- Front lines
- Arno Line
- Lines of defence

Parma

Bologna

Ravenna

La Spezia

Futa Pass

Rimini

Florence

Pesaro

Leghorn

Ancona

Aug 26

POL II CORPS

Albert Line

Chienti

Aso

Elba

Tronto

June 17

Orvieto

US IV CORPS

10th ARMY (General von Vietinghof)

L'Aquila

Bolsena

Tiber

Terni

June 9

Pescara

FR EXP CORPS

TYRRHENIAN SEA

June 5

ROME

US II CORPS

BRIT X CORPS

8th ARMY (General Leese)

US VI CORPS

5th ARMY (General Clark)

Cassino

Anzio

Miles
0    20    40    60

0   20   40   60   80  100
Kilometers

**TOP LEFT:** North American P-51 Mustang fighters of the USAAF. Powered by Packard-built Merlin V-1650-3 engines they were superb fighters and ground attack aircraft.

**ABOVE:** USAAF Martin B-26 Marauders of the 12th Air Force attack railway yards in Milan interdicting German reinforcements and re-supply operations. Marauders had a bomb load of 1,814kg (4,000lb).

**RIGHT:** Florentine citizens make their way carefully across one of the historic bridges on the Arno demolished by the Germans as they pulled back to the Gothic Line.

and deep river valleys. Also the grim winter weather produced many ribald jokes about "Sunny Italy".

Besides the Albert Line the Germans had established blocking positions on the main roads from Rome to Sienna and from Perugia

**ABOVE:** *Gebirgsjäger* with an MG34 in an AA role. Tracer would allow the gunner to correct his aim against aircraft and the stone built position would be hard to detect from the air.

**FAR RIGHT:** A paratrooper looks through the embrasure of his roughly constructed position. An MG42 machine gun is ready to hand along with his MP40 SMG.

**RIGHT:** *Gebirgsjäger* in their distinctive anoraks manoeuvre a 7.5cm *leichte Gebirgs Infrantriegeschutz* 18 into a rocky gun pit. The gun weighed 440kg (970lb) and broke down into ten loads.

**ABOVE:** A British 4 x 2 Light Utility Car makes heavy going on a muddy road better suited for the 4 x 4 Jeeps.

**BELOW:** A US 4.2in (107mm) mortar in action. It was unusual among US mortars, having a rifled barrel, but was muzzle loaded.

**LEFT:** Even Jeeps could be defeated by the mud of "sunny Italy". Here manpower and mechanical horsepower try to extricate a US Army Jeep from conditions that look similar to a road in USSR in the *rasputitsa*.

# FIELD MARSHAL HAROLD ALEXANDER OF TUNIS

Harold Rupert Leofric George Alexander 1st Earl Alexander of Tunis (1891-1969), British field marshal, was born in County Tyrone, Ireland, and educated at the Royal Military College Sandhurst. Following distinguished service as an officer during World War I, he held various positions in the British army, including command of a brigade in India. In 1938 he was appointed major general.

In 1939, after the outbreak of World War II, Alexander commanded the 1st Div in France. Later, as commander of I Corps, he directed the evacuation of the British army from Dunkirk, and was the last soldier to leave France. Appointed commander in chief of British forces in the Middle East in August 1942, he organised the drive on Tunis between October to December. In February 1943 he became Deputy C-in-C, under Eisenhower, of all Allied ground forces in North Africa; later that year he directed the invasions of Sicily and Italy. He succeeded Eisenhower as supreme allied commander in the Mediterranean Theatre of Operations in 1944 and was promoted to the rank of Field

Marshal in November, following the capture of Rome. Eisenhower valued Alexander's diplomatic as well as military talents and wanted him to be his deputy in the invasion of Northern Europe, but was overruled by the British government.

Alexander was Governor-General of Canada from 1946 to 1952 and British Defence Minister from 1952 to 1954 in the Conservative government. He was granted the title of Viscount in 1946 and of Earl in1952 and died in 1969.

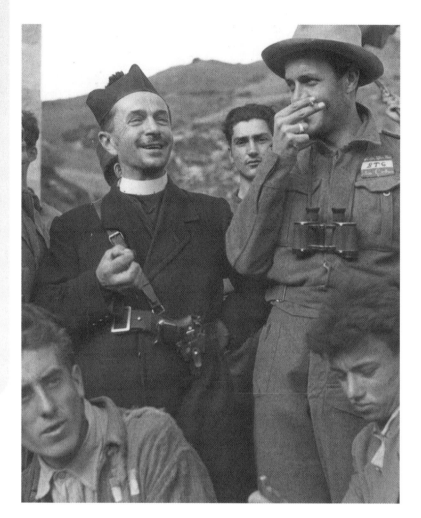

**RIGHT:** An SAS Vickers MMG crew carrying the gun broken down into barrel, tripod and ammunition and water container.

**BELOW RIGHT:** An SAS 3in mortar in action. In Operation Tombola in March 1945. Some fifty men from 3 Squadron 2 SAS under Major Roy Farran, with 70 escaped Russian PoWs and a number of local partisans, armed with a 75mm Pack Howitzer, a 60mm Mortar, an M1A1 2.36in Rocket Launcher and Vickers MMG attacked German supply lines and the German HQ at Albinea.

**ABOVE:** Biretta meets Beretta. An armed Italian priest with a British-equipped and-supplied partisan group operating in mountains in northern Italy.

to Arezo. North of these positions they also established the Arno Line along the valley of the River Arno. In Florence German engineers blew up every bridge across the river Arno, but spared the historic Ponte Vecchio: the Germans fired charges that cratered its approaches and then planted S *Minen* – anti-personnel mines – in the rubble.

The Germans might be masters of the delaying tactics of demolitions, booby traps and minefields, but they had to contend with Allied air attacks and the constant threat of ambush by partisans. While medium bombers struck road and rail communications, fighters attacked convoys and vehicles. Night-time was not cover against the partisans who based themselves in the Apennines and attacked isolated vehicles and small groups of troops. The local resistance also gave invaluable help recovering Allied aircrew whose aircraft had been shot down behind enemy lines.

The first move was Operation Olive, an attack on the right flank along the Adriatic Coast by the three corps, the British V, Canadian I and the Polish II. By August 29 they had reached the Foglia and the Gothic Line. A day later the Canadians managed to break through the defences and reached the River Conca, while the British were held in front of Clemente. Kesselring moved reinforcements to block these moves, and with the aid of heavy autumn rain to help them, brought the attack to a halt.

On September 12 the US II and British XIII Corps were launched against the centre of the Gothic Line high on the Apennines. They were attacking at the junction between the German 10th and 14th Armies just east of the Il Giorgo Pass. On the west coast the US IV Corps kept the pressure on the Germans and

## AXIS SALLY

Born in Portland, Maine, USA in 1901, Mildred Gillars, known to Allied troops as "Axis Sally", was a student drop out from Ohio Wesleyan where in 1920 she was the first woman student to wear trousers. She went to Germany in the 1920s as a music student where she fell in love with her professor at Hunter College. During World War II he persuaded her to broadcast Nazi propaganda to Allied troops who enjoyed her taste in jazz and popular music and found her sexy voice and propaganda rather amusing. She was arrested in 1945 and served 12 years in a Federal prison. After she was released from 1962, she worked as a music teacher at a Catholic girls school in Columbus, Ohio. She died in 1988.

It was widely rumoured in Italy among the soldiers of the 8th Army that the British MP Lady (Nancy) Astor had described these men in this tough and now rather forgotten campaign as "drunken and dissolute D-Day dodgers". She had come to Italy in October 1944 as part of the all Party Parliamentary delegation to examine the troops' living conditions. She denied the slander and even wrote to the Daily Mirror requesting that it publish her denial, but the phrase stuck. To the tune of the German song, Lili Marlene, soldiers slogged down the muddy or dusty roads of Italy sang:

We are the D-Day Dodgers out in Italy,
Always on the vino always on the spree;
Eighth Army scroungers and their tanks,
We go to war in ties like swanks
For we are the D-Day Dodgers, in sunny Italy

We landed at Salerno, a holiday with pay.
Jerry brought his bands out to cheer us on our way,
Showed us the sights and gave us tea,
We all sang songs, the beer was free.
For we are the D-Day Dodgers, the lads that D-Day dodged.

Palermo and Cassino were taken in our stride,
We did not go to fight there, we just went for the ride.
Anzio and Sangro were just names,
We only went to look for dames,
For we are the D-Day Dodgers, in sunny Italy.

# D-DAY DODGERS

On our way to Florence, we had a
lovely time,
We drove a bus from Rimini, right
through the Gothic Line,
Then on to Bologna we did go,
And went bathing in the River Po,
For we are the D-Day Dodgers, the
lads that D-day dodged.

We hear the boys in France are going
home on leave,
After six months' service, such a
shame they're not relieved,
And we're told to carry on a few more
years
Because our wives don't shed no
tears.
For we are the D-Day Dodgers, out in
sunny Italy.

**ABOVE:** Men of the 2nd Battalion Lancashire Fusiliers rest during the push on Ferraro.

prevented reinforcements moving to the mountains. In the Apennines the Americans became involved in a desperate fight for the two peaks, Montecelli and Monte Altuzzo, that dominated Il Giogo Pass. The features were not secured until September 17.

On the coast the British 8th Army resumed its attacks, and on the night of the 12/13, captured Cariano and looked close to a major breakthrough. The heavy autumn rains, however, prevented tanks from being brought forward and the advance was not resumed until a day later. A week of hard fighting followed and the Germans were forced back to the Rimini Line.

Up in the mountains American troops captured Fiorenzuola on September 21 which presented Kesselring with the threat that they might break through to Route 9. On the

8th Army front the Greek Brigade took Rimini and the Canadians crossed the Marecchia River. The next obstacle was the River Po about 100km (62.1miles) to the north, but there were nine rivers to be assaulted before the 8th Army reached this obstacle.

On September 24 the forces of General Clark advanced towards Bologna. The German Army had fought hard but by September 27 it appeared that the Allies were through the Gothic Line.

By October 7 the 8th Army began to attack towards the River Rubicon and in five days were across this symbolic river. General Sir

**BELOW:** US Military Police guard a group of German PoWs. One soldier, a *Panzergrenadier*, wears a uniform made from Italian camouflaged material similar to that shown on page 76.

**ABOVE:** USAAF Consolidated B-24D Liberator bombers fly over the Italian Alps to attack targets in Austria and southern Germany. The Liberator could carry a maximum bomb load of 3,992kg (8,800lb).

Henry Maitland Wilson, the Allied Mediterranean C-in-C sent congratulations saying: "I hope that the crossing of the Rubicon will lead, as with a famous commander in the past, to a decisive victory and the destruction of Kesselring's army."

At the end of October, in the mountains, the 5th Army closed down its offensive. In a month it had suffered 15,700 casualties and was not out of the mountains.

On November 24 Clark handed command of the US 5th Army to General Truscott and succeeded Alexander as the C-in-C of the 15th Army Group and so command of Allied ground forces in Italy. Alexander was promoted to Supreme Allied Commander in the Mediterranean.

On the coast the advance continued.

Canadian troops occupied Ravenna on December 5. Fighting slowed down with the onset of winter. The 8th Army reached the line of the River Senio south of Lake Comacchio by December 29.

Kesselring had considered that the valleys of the Rivers Po and the Adige could be used as intermediate defence lines as his forces fell back to strong positions in the southern Alps. Both he and Alexander knew that it would be hard to dislodge German forces in the mountains. With short supply lines and strong positions they could fight for months. The British general knew that it was critical therefore to keep the pressure on the Germans.

In Berlin Hitler refused to give Kesselring permission to withdraw and insisted that Army Group C should stand and fight. It was the same irrational passion not to give ground to the allied offensive that would see German Armies destroyed on the west bank of the Rhine in 1945.

**ABOVE:** German engineers chisel away flag stones to make holes for Teller anti-tank mines in a narrow street in Florence.

**LEFT:** A PzKpfw V Panther Ausf D. One crewman appears to be an anti-aircraft look out scanning the sky.

**RIGHT:** A *Fallschirmjäger* fires an 8.8cm *Racketen Panzerbüchse* anti-tank weapon, based on captured US Army 60mm "bazooka". Its larger calibre made it more effective and capable of penetrating 100mm armour. It entered service in 1943.

**ABOVE:** General Mark Clark savours his moment of fame in Rome in June 1944. However, all glory is fleeting and within days D-Day had become the front page news.

# INDEX

Adriatic, 77, 79, 88
Aegean, 22, 44, 46
*Afrika Korps*, 4, 7, 10,11, 13, 15, 16, 18, 19, 25, 26, 27, 30, 70
Air Force, 12th, 29, 81
Air Force, 15th, 30
Alban Hills, 70
Albert Line, 79, 81
Alexander, General H, 11, 18, 19, 25, 37, 55, 57, 66, 73, 78, 85, 91, 93
Algeria, 19, 26
Algiers, 21, 26
Alinda Bay, 48, 52
Alps, 91, 93
Ambrosio, General, 26
Anders, General W, 76
Anderson, General K, 25
*Ansaldo* 90/53 *Semovente*, 24
Anzio, 4, 22, 41, 60, 62, 64, 65, 67, 70, 71, 74, 75, 76
Anzio Annie, 57
Appenines, 31, 41, 42, 54, 76, 78, 88, 90
Appetici, 52
Arnim, General J von, 21, 22, 23, 25, 26
Arno, 81, 86
Army Italian, 7, 46
Army Panzer 1st, 60
Army US 1st, 13, 22, 25, 26
Army British 2nd, 13
Army US 3rd, 16
Army US 5th, 25, 55, 60, 76, 91
Army Panzer 5th, 21, 25
Army Italian 6th, 35
Army US 6th, 55
Army US 7th, 28, 35, 37
Army 8th, 4, 6, 8, 9, 12,13, 16, 19, 25, 26, 32, 35, 38, 39, 40, 41, 55, 60, 90, 93
Army 10th German, 40, 54, 56, 75, 88
Army 14th German, 60, 70, 75, 88
Army 18th, 25
Army US 15th, 16
Army Group C, 93
Army Group 15th, 37, 91
Army Group 21st, 13
Astor, Lady, 88
Atlantic, 30
Austria, 16, 31, 55, 91
Avalanche, Operation, 32, 40
Axis, 5, 12, 16, 26
Axis Sally, 88
B-17, Boeing, 33, 64
B-24 Liberator, 91
B-26 Martin Marauder, 64, 81

B-125, 64
Baade, General, 63
Badoglio, Marshal P, 41, 46
Battalion 1st FJR 2, 50

Battalion 1st Durham Light Infantry, 45, 50
Battalion 1st Kings Own Royal Regiment, 48, 51
Battalion 2nd Royal Irish Fusiliers, 48, 51, 52
Battalion 4th Royal West Kents, 48, 51, 52
Battalion 11th The Parachute Regiment, 45
Battery 3rd Light RA, 49
Baytown, Operation, 32, 40
Bavaria, 29, 43
Beaufighter, T.F. Mk X, Bristol, 21
Berlin, 10, 93
Bernhard Line, 55
Bersaglieri, 27
Bf109, Messerschmitt, 14, 15, 38, 46, 49
Bizerta, 26, 27
Bofors 40mm, 49, 52
Bou Arada, 26
Bradley, General O, 37
Bren Gun carrier, 45, 68
Brigade, 1st Airlanding, 37
Brigade 6th New Zealand, 69
Brigade, 18th Coastal, 37
Brigade Greek, 90
Brigade 24th Guards, 72
Brittorous, Maj General F, 51

Camare Bay, 50
Campioni, Admiral, 45
Canadian forces, 40, 78, 88
Cape Bon, 26
Caporetto, 46
Capri, Operation, 26
Carden-Loyd, 68
Cariano, 90
Carroceto, 72, 74
Castle Hill, 68
Catania, 37
Cattolica, 77
Chienti, 79
Churchill, 4, 5, 18, 19, 27, 44, 70, 78
Cisterna, 72
Clark, General M, 40, 41, 55, 70, 76, 77, 90, 91, 95
Clemente, 88
Clidi Bay, 52
Clidi Mount, 52
Cohen, Jack, 34
Comacchio, 93
Commandos, 40
Conca, 88
Corps I *Fallschirm*, 72
Corps I Canadian, 88
Corps II, 23, 26, 37, 56, 60, 75, 88
Corps II New Zealand, 64
Corps II Polish, 76, 88
Corps IV, 88
Corps V, 55, 88
Corps VI, 40, 69, 70, 74, 75
Corps X, 10, 40, 60
Corps XIII, 11, 38, 41, 88
Corps XIV *Panzer*, 38

Corps XX, 7
Corps XXI, 7
Corps XXX, 10, 38
Corps LXXVI *Panzer*, 72
Corsica, 49
Crete, 17, 49

Darlan, Admiral F, 21
Darmstadt, 42
Dawley, General E, 40
DC3, Douglas Dakota, 46
D-Day, 13, 88, 95
D-Day Dodgers, 88
Dempsey, General M, 38
DFS 230, 41
Diadem, Operation, 76
Diamere, Abbot G, 58, 66
Division 1st, 33, 38, 69, 70, 72, 74, 85
Division 1st Airborne, 40, 41
Division 1st Armoured, 10
Division 1st Canadian, 57
Division 1st *Fallschirmjäger*, 63, 73
Division 1st South African, 10
Division 3rd, 13, 39, 55, 69, 70, 74
Division 4th, 66, 76
Division 4th Indian, 69
Division 6th Armoured, 26
Division 8th Indian, 76
Division 9th Australian, 10, 15
Division 10th Armoured, 10
Division 10th Panzer, 26
Division, 15th *Panzergrenadier*, 35
Division 16th *Panzer*, 40
Division 21st *Panzer*, 10, 12
Division 29th *Panzergrenadier*, 40
Division 34th, 60
Division 36th, 64
Division 51st Highland, 10
Division 56th, 55
Division 71st, 76
Division 82nd Airborne, 41
Division 90th Light, 9
Division 90th *Panzergrenadier*, 63
Division 164th, 9
Division 204 Coastal, 38
Division 207 Coastal, 38
Division, *Ariete*, 10, 12
Division, *Bologna*, 9
Division *Brescia*, 9
Division *Waffen-SS Das Reich*, 42
Division, *Folgore*, 9, 11
Division, *Hermann Göring*, 35, 38, 66
Division, *Littorio*, 9
Division, *Nembo*, 32
Division, New Zealand, 10, 69
Division, *Pavia*, 9
Division, *Trento*, 9
Dodecanese, 44, 45, 46, 49, 53

Dolbe, Major, 45
*Duce*, 43
DUKW, 65
Dunkirk, 13, 85
DSO, 13

Eastern Front, 30, 39
*Egret*, HMS, 35
Eisenhower, General D, 26, 46, 85
*El Agheila*, 16
El Alamein, 4, 6, 8, 13, 16, 17
El Aouina, 21
Essex Regiment, 69
Ethiopia, 46

*Fallschirmjäger*, 41, 54, 56, 57, 58, 62, 73, 75, 79
Farran, Major R, 86
Feriana, 25
FG 42, 47
Fieseler *Storch*, 43
*Fiorenzuola*, 90
FJR 3, 37
FJR 4, 37
Flail tank, 8
Flak 8.8-cm, 12, 24
Flak 2-cm, 79
Flanders, 29
Florence, 86
Foggia, 78
Foglia, 78, 88
Fondouk, 25
Foreign Legion, 26
France, 49
Fredenhall, General F, 19, 25, 26
French, Lt Colonel M, 51, 52
French Expeditionary Force, 64, 76
Freyberg, General, 64
*Führer*, 15, 16, 43

Gafsa, 23, 25
Garda, Lake, 43
Gargnano, 43
Garigliano, 31, 54, 55, 60
Gazala, 9, 16
*Gebirgsjäger*, 79, 82
Gela, 37, 58
Gibraltar, 48
Gioda, General, 7
Giorgo Pass, 88, 90
Gothic Line, 77, 78, 80, 81, 88, 90
Goumiers, 76
Gran Sasso, 41, 42
Greif, Operation, 42
Grifo Bay, 52
Grosseto, 79
Gurna bay, 52
Gustav Line, 31, 41, 54, 55, 56, 64, 69, 76
Guzzoni, General, 35

Halifax, Handley Page, 49
Hamman Lif, 27
Hangman's Hill, 69
He111, Heinkel, 49

Heidrich, General, 63
Herr, General, 72
Heydrich, Reinhard, 45
Highway 7, 74
Himmler, Heinrich, 45
Hitler, Adolf, 6, 15, 31, 43,
    49, 54, 64, 72, 93
Hitler Line, 77
Horrocks, General B, 11
Horthy, Admiral M, 42
HS-293, Henschel, 35
Hudson, Lockheed, 49
Hurricane Mk IID, Hawker,
    20
Husky, Operation, 28, 35

Italy, 5, 28, 30, 31, 49, 85

Jeep, 35, 84, 85
Jellicoe, Major Earl, 45
Jodl, General, 28
Ju52, Junkers, 21, 51, 52
Ju87, Junkers, 49
Ju88, Junkers, 46, 49
Ju188, Junkers, 41
July Plot, 42

K5E, 57
K18, 25
Kaltenbrunner, Ernst, 45
Kasserine Pass, 22, 25, 26
Keitel, Field Marshal, 31
Kenyon, Col L.R., 50
Kesselring, Field Marshal A,
    5, 22, 28, 30, 33, 38, 54,
    65, 70, 76, 79, 88, 90, 91,
    93
Kidney Ridge, 7, 15
"Kiel", Battle Group, 9
Knight's Cross, 18, 30
Kos, 22, 44, 45, 48, 49, 52
Kriegsmarine, 48
KRIPO, 45

Lampedusa, 34, 35
Lancashire Fusiliers, 89
Leese, General O, 10, 38, 60
Lehrgang, Operation, 39
Leibstandarte-SS "Adolf
    Hitler", 42
LeGI 18, 82
LeIG 18,13
Leros, 22, 44, 48
Liberator, Lockheed, 45, 49
Licata, 37
Lightfoot, Operation, 10
Lili Marlene, 88
Linosa, 35
Liri, 76
Longstop Hill, 23
Lucas, General J, 41, 70, 71,
    74
Luftflotte I, 30
Luftwaffe, 7, 26, 28, 29, 30,
    33, 35, 40, 47, 49, 50, 52

M3 Stuart, 10
M4 Sherman, 10, 34, 37, 70
M10 Tank Destroyer, 35, 69
M60, 47

Mackensen, General E von,
    60, 74
Maitland Wilson, General
    Sir H, 90
Mareth Line, 22, 23, 26
Marshall, General G, 55
Malta, 32, 35
Marecchia, 90
Matilda tank, 8
McCreery, General R, 40, 60
Me321, Messerschmitt, 20
Me323, Messerschmitt,
    Gigant, 20, 21
Mediterranean, 16, 20, 22,
    29, 41
Messina, 28, 35, 37, 38, 39
Mersa Matruh, 15
MG34, 82
MG42, 58, 76, 82
Military Police, 22, 27, 41
Mines, 8, 22, 57, 86, 93
Miterirya Ridge, 7,15
Monte Cassino, 5, 31, 54,
    58, 59, 61, 62, 63, 64, 65,
    66, 76
Montgomery, General B, 6,
    9, 12, 15, 17, 28, 38, 39,
    55, 60
Morning Wind, Operation,
    23, 25, 26
Mörser 18, 7, 51
Mortar, 79, 84, 86
Morocco, 16, 19
MP 40, 82
Mules, 31, 56
Müller, Lt General, 49, 52,
    53
Mussolini, 16, 30, 31, 33, 38,
    41, 42, 46

Naples, 40, 41, 59
Navarrini, General, 7
Nazi Party, 42, 45
Nehring, General, 27
Nettuno, 70
New Zealand, 75
Normandy, 16, 77
North Africa, 20, 21, 22

OKW, 45
Olive, Operation, 88
Ortona, 54, 57
Overlord, Operation, 60,77

P-38 Lockheed Lightning,
    18, 21, 29
P-40, Curtiss Warhawk, 32
P-47 Republic Thunderbolt,
    73
P-51, North American
    Mustang, 32, 81
Pak36 (r), 11
Pantalleria, 35
Panzergrenadiere, 56
Patton, General G, 16, 19,
    26, 28, 37, 39
Paulus, Alexander, 76
Pesaro, 77, 78
Po, 90, 93
Point 435, 69
Ponte Vecchio, 86

Primasole, 37
PzKpfw III, 38
PzKpfw IV, 37, 38
PzKpfw V, Panther, 39, 93

Rachi Ridge, 48, 52
Rapido, 60, 62, 76
RAF, 31, 33, 46
Rajput Rifles, 69
Ramcke Fallschirmbrigade,
    9
Rangers, 40, 72
Re 2002, Ariete, 29
Regiment 29th
    Panzergrenadier, 72
Regiment US 143rd, 56
Rhine, 16, 93
Rhodes, 44, 45, 49
Richard, Operation, 70
Ridgeway, General M, 41
Rimini Line, 90
Roma, 35
Rome, 5, 28, 32, 41, 76, 81,
    85, 95
Rommel, Field Marshal E, 6,
    9, 11, 12, 15, 22, 25, 26,
    28, 30
Route 6, 76
Route 9, 90
Royal Engineers, 8
Royal Navy, 35, 50
RSAH, 45
Rubicon, 90, 91
Ruweisat Ridge, 7, 9
Ryder, General C, 19

SAAF, 46
Salerno, 32, 40, 41, 59, 65
Samos, 44, 53
Sangro, 55
Sardinia, 32, 35
SAS, 2nd, 33, 86
Sbeitla, 25
Sbiba, 26
SBS, 45, 46, 50, 52, 53
Schlegel, Lt Colonel J, 66
Schlemm, General, 72
Schupos, 45
SD-1400, Ruhrstahl, 35
Senger und Etterlin,
    General von, 58
Senio, 93
Sfax, 10
SFH 18, 9
Shingle, Operation, 69
Sicherheitsdienst, 45
Sicily, 13, 16, 21, 22, 27, 30,
    32, 33, 37, 39, 65
Sidi Bou Zid, 23, 25
Skorzeny,
    Obersturmbannführer O,
    41
Slapstick, Operation, 32
SMLE, 6, 8, 74
Snapdragon, Operation, 33
Spain, 35, 42
Spitfire, Supermarine, 14, 45
Spring Wind, Operation, 23,
    25
SS, 50

Stalingrad, 76
Staghound, 68
Stalingrad, 27
StuG III, 60, 61
Stumme, General G, 12, 15
Sturmpanzer IV, 72
Supercharge, Operation, 11,
    15

TA-16, 53
Tank destroyer, 69
Task Force Centre, 19, 21
Task Force, Eastern, 19, 21
Task Force, Western, 19
Tebourba, 23
Thala, 26
Tiger Tank, 21, 38
Tobruk, 15
Tombola, Operation, 86
Torch, Operation, 19
Trasimene Lake, 79
Tripoli, 16, 41
Truscot, General L, 57, 74,
    91
Tunis, 26, 85
Tunisia, 10, 16, 16, 21, 23,
    27
Turkey, 5, 45
Typhoon, Hawker, 73

U-Boat, 21, 48
Uganda, HMS, 35
ULTRA, 4, 9, 13, 15, 21, 26,
    50, 70
United Nations, 55
Universal Carrier, 68
USAAF, 18, 21, 30, 31, 34,
    64, 73
US Army, 42
US Navy, 35
USSR, 45

Vaerst, General G von, 27
Valetta, 35
Vallo di Lucania, 41
Vickers MMG, 86
Victor Emmanuel, King, 41
Vietinghoff, General H von,
    40
Volturno, 55

Wadi Akarit, 23
Waffen-SS, 42, 43, 66
Warspite, HMS, 35
Wellington, Vickers, 49
Western Front, 29, 64
Winter Line, 54
World War I, 13,16, 29, 46,
    60, 64, 75, 85
World War II, 16, 55, 60, 72